Either you decide to stay in the shallow end of the pool or you go out in the ocean.

Christopher Reeve

Your time is limited, so don't waste it living someone else's life. Don't be trapped by dogma - which is living with the results of other people's thinking. Don't let the noise of others' opinions drown out your own inner voice. And most important, have the courage to follow your heart and intuition.

Steve Jobs

Courage is what it takes to stand up and speak; courage is also what it takes to sit down and listen.

Winston Churchill

He who is not courageous enough to take risks will accomplish nothing in life.

Muhammad Ali

I learned that courage was not the absence of fear, but the triumph over it. The brave man is not he who does not feel afraid, but he who conquers that fear.

Nelson Mandela

Only those who will risk going too far can possibly find out how far one can go.

T. S. Eliot

The greatest test of courage on earth is to bear defeat without losing heart.

Robert Green Ingersoll

You gain strength, courage, and confidence by every experience in which you really stop to look fear in the face. You are able to say to yourself, 'I lived through this horror. I can take the next thing that comes along.'

Eleanor Roosevelt

Courage is being scared to death... and saddling up anyway.

John Wayne

You will never do anything in this world without courage. It is the greatest quality of the mind next to honor.

Aristotle

It takes a great deal of bravery to stand up to our enemies, but just as much to stand up to our friends.

J. K. Rowling

Let us not pray to be sheltered from dangers but to be fearless when facing them.

Rabindranath Tagore

One isn't necessarily born with courage, but one is born with potential. Without courage, we cannot practice any other virtue with consistency. We can't be kind, true, merciful, generous, or honest.

Maya Angelou

Don't Make Assumptions. Find the courage to ask questions and to express what you really want. Communicate with others as clearly as you can to avoid misunderstandings, sadness and drama. With just this one agreement, you can completely transform your life.

Miguel Angel Ruiz

My message, especially to young people is to have courage to think differently, courage to invent, to travel the unexplored path, courage to discover the impossible and to conquer the problems and succeed. These are great qualities that they must work towards. This is my message to the young people.

A. P. J. Abdul Kalam

Efforts and courage are not enough without purpose and direction.

John F. Kennedy

Courageous people do not fear forgiving, for the sake of peace.

Nelson Mandela

Loyalty and devotion lead to bravery. Bravery leads to the spirit of self-sacrifice. The spirit of self-sacrifice creates trust in the power of love.

Morihei Ueshiba

We must become bigger than we have been: more courageous, greater in spirit, larger in outlook. We must become members of a new race, overcoming petty prejudice, owing our ultimate allegiance not to nations but to our fellow men within the human community.

Haile Selassie

Bravery is the capacity to perform properly even when scared half to death.

Omar N. Bradley

Courage is grace under pressure.

Ernest Hemingway

Have no fear of moving into the unknown. Simply step out fearlessly knowing that I am with you, therefore no harm can befall you; all is very, very well. Do this in complete faith and confidence.

Pope John Paul II

Inaction breeds doubt and fear. Action breeds confidence and courage. If you want to conquer fear, do not sit home and think about it. Go out and get busy.

Dale Carnegie

If you are lucky enough to find a way of life you love, you have to find the courage to live it.

John Irving

Have the courage to say no. Have the courage to face the truth. Do the right thing because it is right. These are the magic keys to living your life with integrity.

W. Clement Stone

Clear thinking requires courage rather than intelligence.

Thomas Szasz

Courage is fire, and bullying is smoke.

Benjamin Disraeli

Courage, above all things, is the first quality of a warrior.

Carl von Clausewitz

We have a powerful potential in out youth, and we must have the courage to change old ideas and practices so that we may direct their power toward good ends.

Mary McLeod Bethune

Men make history and not the other way around. In periods where there is no leadership, society stands still. Progress occurs when courageous, skillful leaders seize the opportunity to change things for the better.

Harry S Truman

The most courageous act is still to think for yourself. Aloud.

Coco Chanel

Courage is not simply one of the virtues, but the form of every virtue at the testing point.

C. S. Lewis

Courage is resistance to fear, mastery of fear, not absence of fear.

Mark Twain

I know of no higher fortitude than stubborness in the face of overwhelming odds.

Louis Nizer

From caring comes courage.

Lao Tzu

Who could refrain that had a heart to love and in that heart courage to make love known?

William Shakespeare

Courage is the price that life exacts for granting peace.

Amelia Earhart

The eagle has no fear of adversity. We need to be like the eagle and have a fearless spirit of a conqueror!

Joyce Meyer

Those who lack the courage will always find a philosophy to justify it.

Albert Camus

Creativity requires the courage to let go of certainties.

Erich Fromm

The greatest obstacle to being heroic is the doubt whether one may not be going to prove one's self a fool; the truest heroism is to resist the doubt; and the profoundest wisdom, to know when it ought to be resisted, and when it be obeyed.

Nathaniel Hawthorne

If you could get up the courage to begin, you have the courage to succeed.

David Viscott

Failure is unimportant. It takes courage to make a fool of

yourself.

Charlie Chaplin

It takes a lot of courage to release the familiar and seemingly secure, to embrace the new. But there is no real security in what is no longer meaningful. There is more security in the adventurous and exciting, for in movement there is life, and in change there is power.

Alan Cohen

Success is never final, failure is never fatal. It's courage that counts.

John Wooden

There are a group of people who would like to silence everybody and have everybody go along to get along, but that's not going to be very helpful for us in the long run, in terms of solving our problems. And somebody has to be courageous enough to actually stand up to, you know, the bullies.

Benjamin Carson

There are no easy answers, but there are simple answers. We must have the courage to do what we know is morally right.

Ronald Reagan

We must build dikes of courage to hold back the flood of fear.

Martin Luther King, Jr.

Courage is the capacity to confront what can be imagined.

Leo Rosten

Always be courageous and strong, and don't fear.

Gabby Douglas

Courage is never to let your actions be influenced by your fears.

Arthur Koestler

What would life be if we had no courage to attempt

anything?

Vincent Van Gogh

Man cannot discover new oceans unless he has the courage to lose sight of the shore.

Andre Gide

I think my mother... made it clear that you have to live life by your own terms and you have to not worry about what other people think and you have to have the courage to do the unexpected.

Caroline Kennedy

Real courage is when you know you're licked before you begin, but you begin anyway and see it through no matter what.

Harper Lee

Courage is fear holding on a minute longer.

George S. Patton

Any intelligent fool can make things bigger and more complex... It takes a touch of genius - and a lot of courage to move in the opposite direction.

E. F. Schumacher

The opposite for courage is not cowardice, it is conformity. Even a dead fish can go with the flow.

Jim Hightower

The best protection any woman can have... is courage.

Elizabeth Cady Stanton

Courage is found in unlikely places.

J. R. R. Tolkien

God, give us grace to accept with serenity the things that cannot be changed, courage to change the things which should be changed and the wisdom to distinguish the one from the other.

Reinhold Niebuhr

Courage is doing what you are afraid to do. There can be no courage unless you are scared.

Eddie Rickenbacker

Life is to be entered upon with courage.

Alexis de Tocqueville

The opposite of courage in our society is not cowardice, it is conformity.

Rollo May

Courage is the most important of all the virtues, because without courage you can't practice any other virtue consistently. You can practice any virtue erratically, but nothing consistently without courage.

Maya Angelou

People say to me all the time, 'You have no fear.' I tell them, 'No, that's not true. I'm scared all the time. You have to have fear in order to have courage. I'm a courageous person because I'm a scared person.'

Ronda Rousey

You have to really be courageous about your instincts and your ideas. Otherwise you'll just knuckle under, and things that might have been memorable will be lost.

Francis Ford Coppola

Life shrinks or expands in proportion to one's courage.

Anais Nin

Never be discouraged. If I were sunk in the lowest pits of Nova Scotia, with the Rocky Mountains piled on me, I would hang on, exercise faith, and keep up good courage, and I would come out on top.

Joseph Smith, Jr.

How few there are who have courage enough to own their faults, or resolution enough to mend them.

Benjamin Franklin

Courage is not the absence of despair; it is, rather, the capacity to move ahead in spite of despair.

Rollo May

Fate loves the fearless.

James Russell Lowell

Faced with what is right, to leave it undone shows a lack of courage.

Confucius

Courage is the greatest of all virtues, because if you haven't courage, you may not have an opportunity to use any of the others.

Samuel Johnson

True courage is being afraid, and going ahead and doing your job anyhow, that's what courage is.

Norman Schwarzkopf

The courage to be is the courage to accept oneself, in spite of being unacceptable.

Paul Tillich

One man with courage is a majority.

Thomas Jefferson

It is only necessary to have courage, for strength without self-confidence is useless.

Giacomo Casanova

The minute a person whose word means a great deal to others dare to take the open-hearted and courageous way, many others follow.

Marian Anderson

He is a man of courage who does not run away, but remains at his post and fights against the enemy.

Socrates

Courage is the ladder on which all the other virtues mount.

Clare Boothe Luce

The only service a friend can really render is to keep up your courage by holding up to you a mirror in which you can see a noble image of yourself.

George Bernard Shaw

Creativity takes courage.

Henri Matisse

I tend to think you're fearless when you recognize why you should be scared of things, but do them anyway.

Christian Bale

It requires more courage to suffer than to die.

Napoleon Bonaparte

Do not lose courage in considering your own imperfections.

Saint Francis de Sales

Have courage for the great sorrows of life and patience for the small ones; and when you have laboriously accomplished your daily task, go to sleep in peace.

Victor Hugo

A great deal of talent is lost to the world for want of a little courage. Every day sends to their graves obscure men whose timidity prevented them from making a first effort.

Sydney Smith

A timid person is frightened before a danger, a coward during the time, and a courageous person afterward.

Jean Paul

Valor grows by daring, fear by holding back.

Publilius Syrus

People with courage and character always seem sinister to the rest.

Hermann Hesse

The secret to happiness is freedom... And the secret to freedom is courage.

Thucydides

Courage is knowing what not to fear.

Plato

Courage is contagious. When a brave man takes a stand, the spines of others are often stiffened.

Billy Graham

Be courageous. I have seen many depressions in business. Always America has emerged from these stronger and more prosperous. Be brave as your fathers before you. Have faith! Go forward!

Thomas A. Edison

Happy are those who dare courageously to defend what they love.

Ovid

I have a lot of things to prove to myself. One is that I can live my life fearlessly.

Oprah Winfrey

Love bravely, live bravely, be courageous, there's really nothing to lose. There's no wrong you can't make right again, so be kinder to yourself, you know, have fun, take chances. There's no bounds.

Jewel

It requires greater courage to preserve inner freedom, to move on in one's inward journey into new realms, than to stand defiantly for outer freedom. It is often easier to play the martyr, as it is to be rash in battle.

Rollo May

Boldness be my friend.

William Shakespeare

Valor lies just halfway between rashness and cowardice.

Miguel de Cervantes

Courage is being afraid but going on anyhow.

Dan Rather

Fearlessness is not only possible, it is the ultimate joy.
When you touch nonfear, you are free.

Thich Nhat Hanh

We must have courage to bet on our ideas, to take the
calculated risk, and to act. Everyday living requires courage
if life is to be effective and bring happiness.

Maxwell Maltz

I'm grateful to God for His bountiful gifts... He gave me
courage and faith in myself.

Loretta Young

Courage - a perfect sensibility of the measure of danger,
and a mental willingness to endure it.

William Tecumseh Sherman

True courage is not the brutal force of vulgar heroes, but the firm resolve of virtue and reason.

Alfred North Whitehead

Courage is a kind of salvation.

Plato

To have courage for whatever comes in life - everything lies in that.

Saint Teresa of Avila

A lot of people do not muster the courage to live their dreams because they are afraid to die.

Les Brown

The trials on the road to world harmony are no greater than the courage of those who accept the challenge.

Carl Lewis

Courage and conviction are powerful weapons against an enemy who depends only on fists or guns. Animals know when you are afraid; a coward knows when you are not.

David Seabury

Hope, like faith, is nothing if it is not courageous; it is nothing if it is not ridiculous.

Thornton Wilder

I feel quite fearless protecting the people I love.

Paloma Faith

A great part of courage is the courage of having done the thing before.

Ralph Waldo Emerson

Courage is on display every day, and only the courageous wring the most out of life.

Zig Ziglar

The only courage that matters is the kind that gets you from one moment to the next.

Mignon McLaughlin

Everyone has talent. What is rare is the courage to follow the talent to the dark place where it leads.

Erica Jong

Who asks whether the enemy was defeated by strategy or valor?

Virgil

Courage is often lack of insight, whereas cowardice in many cases is based on good information.

Peter Ustinov

You can't test courage cautiously.

Annie Dillard

It's a courageous thing to do something that doesn't have

rules or limits.

Vanessa Paradis

Being deeply loved by someone gives you strength, while loving someone deeply gives you courage.

Lao Tzu

Success is not final, failure is not fatal: it is the courage to continue that counts.

Winston Churchill

All our dreams can come true, if we have the courage to pursue them.

Walt Disney

You don't develop courage by being happy in your relationships everyday. You develop it by surviving difficult times and challenging adversity.

Epicurus

Goodness is about character - integrity, honesty, kindness, generosity, moral courage, and the like. More than anything else, it is about how we treat other people.

Dennis Prager

Mistakes are always forgivable, if one has the courage to admit them.

Bruce Lee

We gain strength, and courage, and confidence by each experience in which we really stop to look fear in the face... we must do that which we think we cannot.

Eleanor Roosevelt

You may not always have a comfortable life and you will not always be able to solve all of the world's problems at once but don't ever underestimate the importance you can have because history has shown us that courage can be contagious and hope can take on a life of its own.

Michelle Obama

My great hope is to laugh as much as I cry; to get my work

done and try to love somebody and have the courage to accept the love in return.

Maya Angelou

Vulnerability is the essence of romance. It's the art of being uncalculated, the willingness to look foolish, the courage to say, 'This is me, and I'm interested in you enough to show you my flaws with the hope that you may embrace me for all that I am but, more important, all that I am not.'

Ashton Kutcher

A grateful heart is a beginning of greatness. It is an expression of humility. It is a foundation for the development of such virtues as prayer, faith, courage, contentment, happiness, love, and well-being.

James E. Faust

God grant me the serenity to accept the things I cannot change, the courage to change the things I can, and the wisdom to know the difference.

Reinhold Niebuhr

Life is the most exciting opportunity we have. But we have one shot. You graduate from college once, and that's it. You're going out of that nest. And you have to find that courage that's deep, deep, deep in there. Every step of the way.

Andrew Shue

Character contributes to beauty. It fortifies a woman as her youth fades. A mode of conduct, a standard of courage, discipline, fortitude, and integrity can do a great deal to make a woman beautiful.

Jacqueline Bisset

You can't forgive without loving. And I don't mean sentimentality. I don't mean mush. I mean having enough courage to stand up and say, 'I forgive. I'm finished with it.'

Maya Angelou

Courage, sacrifice, determination, commitment, toughness, heart, talent, guts. That's what little girls are made of.

Bethany Hamilton

It takes courage to grow up and become who you really are.

e. e. cummings

I think we judge talent wrong. What do we see as talent? I think I have made the same mistake myself. We judge talent by people's ability to strike a cricket ball. The sweetness, the timing. That's the only thing we see as talent. Things like determination, courage, discipline, temperament, these are also talent.

Rahul Dravid

America was not built on fear. America was built on courage, on imagination and an unbeatable determination to do the job at hand.

Harry S Truman

It is only through labor and painful effort, by grim energy and resolute courage, that we move on to better things.

Theodore Roosevelt

One individual can begin a movement that turns the tide of history. Martin Luther King in the civil rights movement,

Mohandas Ganhi in India, Nelson Mandela in South Africa are examples of people standing up with courage and non-violence to bring about needed changes.

Jack Canfield

Hope lies in dreams, in imagination, and in the courage of those who dare to make dreams into reality.

Jonas Salk

Optimism is essential to achievement and it is also the foundation of courage and true progress.

Nicholas M. Butler

I, with a deeper instinct, choose a man who compels my strength, who makes enormous demands on me, who does not doubt my courage or my toughness, who does not believe me naive or innocent, who has the courage to treat me like a woman.

Anais Nin

Heroes represent the best of ourselves, respecting that we are human beings. A hero can be anyone from Gandhi to your classroom teacher, anyone who can show courage when faced with a problem. A hero is someone who is willing to help others in his or her best capacity.

Ricky Martin

Wisdom, compassion, and courage are the three universally recognized moral qualities of men.

Confucius

Courage means to keep working a relationship, to continue seeking solutions to difficult problems, and to stay focused during stressful periods.

Denis Waitley

All you need is the plan, the road map, and the courage to press on to your destination.

Earl Nightingale

When we tackle obstacles, we find hidden reserves of courage and resilience we did not know we had. And it is only when we are faced with failure do we realise that these resources were always there within us. We only need to find them and move on with our lives.

A. P. J. Abdul Kalam

Success is not measured by what you accomplish, but by the opposition you have encountered, and the courage with which you have maintained the struggle against overwhelming odds.

Orison Swett Marden

The terrorists thought they would change my aims and stop my ambitions, but nothing changed in my life except this: weakness, fear and hopelessness died. Strength, power and courage were born.

Malala Yousafzai

A man of courage is also full of faith.

Marcus Tullius Cicero

Half a century ago, the amazing courage of Rosa Parks, the visionary leadership of Martin Luther King, and the inspirational actions of the civil rights movement led politicians to write equality into the law and make real the promise of America for all her citizens.

David Cameron

You have to accept whatever comes and the only important thing is that you meet it with courage and with the best that you have to give.

Eleanor Roosevelt

The truth is: Belonging starts with self-acceptance. Your level of belonging, in fact, can never be greater than your level of self-acceptance, because believing that you're enough is what gives you the courage to be authentic, vulnerable and imperfect.

Brene Brown

There can be no failure to a man who has not lost his courage, his character, his self respect, or his self-confidence. He is still a King.

Orison Swett Marden

Courtesy is as much a mark of a gentleman as courage.

Theodore Roosevelt

I saw courage both in the Vietnam War and in the struggle to stop it. I learned that patriotism includes protest, not just military service.

John F. Kerry

Genius is talent set on fire by courage.

Henry Van Dyke

My mother taught me about the power of inspiration and courage, and she did it with a strength and a passion that I wish could be bottled.

Carly Fiorina

History, despite its wrenching pain, cannot be unlived, but if faced with courage, need not be lived again.

Maya Angelou

Earth teach me to forget myself as melted snow forgets its life. Earth teach me resignation as the leaves which die in the fall. Earth teach me courage as the tree which stands all alone. Earth teach me regeneration as the seed which rises in the spring.

William Alexander

Soldiers, when committed to a task, can't compromise. It's unrelenting devotion to the standards of duty and courage, absolute loyalty to others, not letting the task go until it's been done.

John Keegan

Courage and perseverance have a magical talisman, before which difficulties disappear and obstacles vanish into air.

John Quincy Adams

The principles of living greatly include the capacity to face trouble with courage, disappointment with cheerfulness, and trial with humility.

Thomas S. Monson

In the Soviet army it takes more courage to retreat than advance.

Joseph Stalin

Honest conviction is my courage; the Constitution is my guide.

Andrew Johnson

The first virtue in a soldier is endurance of fatigue; courage is only the second virtue.

Napoleon Bonaparte

Amongst the qualities a hero should have, I would include determination, loyalty, courage, perseverance, patience, focus, intrepidity and selflessness.

Ricky Martin

It took me realizing that a broken heart has never actually killed anyone to find the courage to ask for what I want, in just about every situation. That was part of my own growing up.

Ginnifer Goodwin

Let us go forth with fear and courage and rage to save the world.

Grace Paley

A wise woman recognizes when her life is out of balance and summons the courage to act to correct it, she knows the meaning of true generosity, happiness is the reward for a life lived in harmony, with a courage and grace.

Suze Orman

The courage of life is often a less dramatic spectacle than the courage of a final moment; but it is no less a magnificent mixture of triumph and tragedy.

John F. Kennedy

We want deeper sincerity of motive, a greater courage in speech and earnestness in action.

Sarojini Naidu

It takes a lot of courage to show your dreams to someone else.

Erma Bombeck

To create one's world in any of the arts takes courage.

Georgia O'Keeffe

Two qualities are indispensable: first, an intellect that, even in the darkest hour, retains some glimmerings of the inner light which leads to truth; and second, the courage to follow this faint light wherever it may lead.

Carl von Clausewitz

Competing at the highest level is not about winning. It's about preparation, courage, understanding and nurturing your people, and heart. Winning is the result.

Joe Torre

A lot of people ask me, 'How did you have the courage to walk up to record labels when you were 12 or 13 and jump right into the music industry?' It's because I knew I could never feel the kind of rejection that I felt in middle school. Because in the music industry, if they're gonna say no to you, at least they're gonna be polite about it.

Taylor Swift

One of the greatest gifts my father gave me -
unintentionally - was witnessing the courage with which he
bore adversity. We had a bit of a rollercoaster life with
some really challenging financial periods. He was always
unshaken, completely tranquil, the same ebullient,
laughing, jovial man.

Ben Okri

We know the threats - from global terrorist networks to the
spread of deadly weapons. Yet we also know that
embedded in this time of danger is the promise of a new
day, if we have the courage and commitment to work
together.

Valerie Jarrett

Love and peace of mind do protect us. They allow us to
overcome the problems that life hands us. They teach us to
survive... to live now... to have the courage to confront each
day.

Bernie Siegel

A team is where a boy can prove his courage on his own. A
gang is where a coward goes to hide.

Mickey Mantle

Physical bravery is an animal instinct; moral bravery is much higher and truer courage.

Wendell Phillips

God grant me the courage not to give up what I think is right even though I think it is hopeless.

Chester W. Nimitz

Because with courage and conviction I believe we can deliver a more flexible, adaptable and open European Union in which the interests and ambitions of all its members can be met.

David Cameron

My mother always taught us that if people don't agree with you, the important thing is to listen to them. But if you've listened to them carefully and you still think that you're right, then you must have the courage of your convictions.

Jane Goodall

Courage to be is the key to revelatory power of the feminist revolution.

Mary Daly

Freedom is the sure possession of those alone who have the courage to defend it.

Pericles

Sailing a boat calls for quick action, a blending of feeling with the wind and water as well as with the very heart and soul of the boat itself. Sailing teaches alertness and courage, and gives in return a joyousness and peace that but few sports afford.

George Matthew Adams

There are no greater treasures than the highest human qualities such as compassion, courage and hope. Not even tragic accident or disaster can destroy such treasures of the heart.

Daisaku Ikeda

The preservation of peace and the guaranteeing of man's basic freedoms and rights require courage and eternal vigilance: courage to speak and act - and if necessary, to suffer and die - for truth and justice; eternal vigilance, that the least transgression of international morality shall not go undetected and unremedied.

Haile Selassie

Presumption should never make us neglect that which appears easy to us, nor despair make us lose courage at the sight of difficulties.

Benjamin Banneker

Courage is the first of human qualities because it is the quality which guarantees the others.

Aristotle

War alone brings up to their highest tension all human energies and imposes the stamp of nobility upon the peoples who have the courage to make it.

Benito Mussolini

Values are principles and ideas that bring meaning to the seemingly mundane experience of life. A meaningful life that ultimately brings happiness and pride requires you to respond to temptations as well as challenges with honor, dignity, and courage.

Laura Schlessinger

Take chances, make mistakes. That's how you grow. Pain nourishes your courage. You have to fail in order to practice being brave.

Mary Tyler Moore

I think we all have empathy. We may not have enough courage to display it.

Maya Angelou

Time is neutral and does not change things. With courage and initiative, leaders change things.

Jesse Jackson

The test of courage comes when we are in the minority. The test of tolerance comes when we are in the majority.

Ralph W. Sockman

There is hope in dreams, imagination, and in the courage of those who wish to make those dreams a reality.

Jonas Salk

The British were indeed very far superior to the Americans in every respect necessary to military operations, except the revivified courage and resolution, the result of sudden success after despair.

Mercy Otis Warren

Collaboration is just, really, a group of people getting in a room with their eye on a very similar prize and wanting to come out with the same show. The director, ultimately, is the guy in front of whom the buck stops. So, he has to have the courage to prevail. But, he has got to have a huge amount of respect for his collaborators.

Harold Prince

Daring to set boundaries is about having the courage to love ourselves, even when we risk disappointing others.

Brene Brown

Do you really think it is weakness that yields to temptation?
I tell you that there are terrible temptations which it
requires strength, strength and courage to yield to.

Oscar Wilde

You will always be fond of me. I represent to you all the
sins you have never had the courage to commit.

Oscar Wilde

Above all, we must realize that no arsenal, or no weapon in
the arsenals of the world, is so formidable as the will and
moral courage of free men and women. It is a weapon our
adversaries in today's world do not have.

Ronald Reagan

I'm a big fan of small business ownership. I think it's the
backbone of American innovation. But to be successful,
you first have to have the courage to go for it.

Bill Rancic

I know that if I'd had to go and take an exam for acting, I

wouldn't have got anywhere. You don't take exams for acting, you take your courage.

Edith Evans

Don't wish me happiness - I don't expect to be happy it's gotten beyond that, somehow. Wish me courage and strength and a sense of humor - I will need them all.

Anne Morrow Lindbergh

I want to grow old without facelifts. I want to have the courage to be loyal to the face I have made.

Marilyn Monroe

One man scorned and covered with scars still strove with his last ounce of courage to reach the unreachable stars; and the world will be better for this.

Miguel de Cervantes

The best thing to do is stare it in the face and move on. We have to face our fears and plow through. I think taking chances takes a lot more courage than staying stagnant and doing what's safe and comfortable.

Terri Clark

There is in true beauty, as in courage, something which
narrow souls cannot dare to admire.

William Congreve

The only reason I'm in Hollywood is that I don't have the
moral courage to refuse the money.

Marlon Brando

The difficult thing is that vulnerability is the first thing I
look for in you and the last thing I'm willing to show you.
In you, it's courage and daring. In me, it's weakness.

Brene Brown

Most of us have far more courage than we ever dreamed we
possessed.

Dale Carnegie

My message to you all is of hope, courage and confidence.
Let us mobilize all our resources in a systematic and

organized way and tackle the grave issues that confront us with grim determination and discipline worthy of a great nation.

Muhammad Ali Jinnah

Healing takes courage, and we all have courage, even if we have to dig a little to find it.

Tori Amos

Courage, not compromise, brings the smile of God's approval.

Thomas S. Monson

Courage! I have shown it for years; think you I shall lose it at the moment when my sufferings are to end?

Marie Antoinette

In general, questions are fine; you can always seize upon the parts of them that interest you and concentrate on answering those. And one has to remember when answering questions that asking questions isn't easy either, and for someone who's quite shy to stand up in an audience to speak takes some courage.

Vikram Seth

Courage is like love; it must have hope for nourishment.

Napoleon Bonaparte

The kind of beauty I want most is the hard-to-get kind that comes from within - strength, courage, dignity.

Ruby Dee

I beg you take courage; the brave soul can mend even disaster.

Catherine the Great

It is curious that physical courage should be so common in the world and moral courage so rare.

Mark Twain

Why should we honour those that die upon the field of battle? A man may show as reckless a courage in entering into the abyss of himself.

William Butler Yeats

The amount of eccentricity in a society has generally been proportional to the amount of genius, mental vigor, and moral courage it contained. That so few now dare to be eccentric marks the chief danger of the time.

John Stuart Mill

The sea - this truth must be confessed - has no generosity. No display of manly qualities - courage, hardihood, endurance, faithfulness - has ever been known to touch its irresponsible consciousness of power.

Joseph Conrad

Leaders come in many forms, with many styles and diverse qualities. There are quiet leaders and leaders one can hear in the next county. Some find strength in eloquence, some in judgment, some in courage.

John W. Gardner

Virtues, like viruses, have their seasons of contagion. When catastrophe strikes, generosity spikes like a fever. Courage spreads in the face of tyranny.

Nancy Gibbs

He who loses wealth loses much; he who loses a friend loses more; but he that loses his courage loses all.

Miguel de Cervantes

But steel bars have never yet kept out a mob; it takes something a good deal stronger: human courage backed up by the consciousness of being right.

Ray Stannard Baker

The presidents of colleges have to have some courage to step forward. You can't limit alcohol in college sports, you have to get rid of it.

Dean Smith

Courage: Great Russian word, fit for the songs of our children's children, pure on their tongues, and free.

Anna Akhmatova

Courage, my friends; 'tis not too late to build a better world.

Tommy Douglas

Failure is only postponed success as long as courage 'coaches' ambition. The habit of persistence is the habit of victory.

Herbert Kaufman

Courage is rightly esteemed the first of human qualities... because it is the quality which guarantees all others.

Winston Churchill

No matter what you think about the Iraq war, there is one thing we can all agree on for the next days - we have to salute the courage and bravery of those who are risking their lives to vote and those brave Iraqi and American soldiers fighting to protect their right to vote.

Hillary Clinton

You have to develop ways so that you can take up for yourself, and then you take up for someone else. And so sooner or later, you have enough courage to really stand up for the human race and say, 'I'm a representative.'

Maya Angelou

It is courage, courage, courage, that raises the blood of life to crimson splendor. Live bravely and present a brave front to adversity.

Horace

There's only one requirement of any of us, and that is to be courageous. Because courage, as you might know, defines all other human behavior. And, I believe - because I've done a little of this myself - pretending to be courageous is just as good as the real thing.

David Letterman

We have to confront ourselves. Do we like what we see in the mirror? And, according to our light, according to our understanding, according to our courage, we will have to say yea or nay - and rise!

Maya Angelou

Every man has his own courage, and is betrayed because he seeks in himself the courage of other persons.

Ralph Waldo Emerson

The principal act of courage is to endure and withstand dangers doggedly rather than to attack them.

Thomas Aquinas

We've begun to raise daughters more like sons... but few have the courage to raise our sons more like our daughters.

Gloria Steinem

To see what is right and not to do it is want of courage, or of principle.

Confucius

He who knows no hardships will know no hardihood. He who faces no calamity will need no courage. Mysterious though it is, the characteristics in human nature which we love best grow in a soil with a strong mixture of troubles.

Harry Emerson Fosdick

The courage to imagine the otherwise is our greatest resource, adding color and suspense to all our life.

Daniel J. Boorstin

We need the compassion and the courage to change the conditions that support our suffering. Those conditions are things like ignorance, bitterness, negligence, clinging, and holding on.

Sharon Salzberg

Courage is a peculiar kind of fear.

Charles Kennedy

If we bring not the good courage of minds covetous of truth, and truth only, prepared to hear all things, and decide upon all things, according to evidence, we should do more wisely to sit down contented in ignorance, than to bestir ourselves only to reap disappointment.

Frances Wright

September 11, 2001, revealed heroism in ordinary people

who might have gone through their lives never called upon to demonstrate the extent of their courage.

Geraldine Brooks

An able, disinterested, public-spirited press, with trained intelligence to know the right and courage to do it, can preserve that public virtue without which popular government is a sham and a mockery.

Joseph Pulitzer

I many times encountered courage, real courage. Undeniable courage. I've heard it said that that was the highest quality of the human animal. I encountered that many times, in unexpected places. And I have learned to recognize it when I see it.

Dorothea Lange

Stripped of its plot, the 'Iliad' is a scattering of names and biographies of ordinary soldiers: men who trip over their shields, lose their courage or miss their wives. In addition to these, there is a cast of anonymous people: the farmers, walkers, mothers, neighbours who inhabit its similes.

Alice Oswald

Simulated disorder postulates perfect discipline; simulated fear postulates courage; simulated weakness postulates strength.

Lao Tzu

It often takes more courage to change one's opinion than to keep it.

Willy Brandt

Valor is stability, not of legs and arms, but of courage and the soul.

Michel de Montaigne

One of the greatest gifts my father gave me - unintentionally - was witnessing the courage with which he bore adversity.

Ben Okri

Decision is a risk rooted in the courage of being free.

Paul Tillich

Let's drink to the spirit of gallantry and courage that made a strange Heaven out of unbelievable Hell, and let's drink to the hope that one day this country of ours, which we love so much, will find dignity and greatness and peace again.

Noel Coward

Have the courage to act instead of react.

Oliver Wendell Holmes, Sr.

Today we affirm a new commitment to live out our nation's promise through civility, courage, compassion and character.

George W. Bush

'The Impossible Dream' is, in my opinion, one of the greatest songs ever written. Here is a man, an old man, a very old man full of daring, bravery, courage, determination, romanticism and dreams.

Christopher Lee

Being a leader for me is about having the courage to speak

the truth, and live the truth, despite attempts to silence our thoughts, feelings, and past experiences.

Zainab Salbi

Change will never happen when people lack the ability and courage to see themselves for who they are.

Bryant H. McGill

Wisdom, prudence, forethought, these are essential. But not second to these that noble courage which adventures the right, and leaves the consequences to God.

Robert Dale Owen

Just remaining quietly in the presence of God, listening to Him, being attentive to Him, requires a lot of courage and know-how.

Thomas Merton

And I love that even in the toughest moments, when we're all sweating it - when we're worried that the bill won't pass, and it seems like all is lost - Barack never lets himself get distracted by the chatter and the noise. Just like his grandmother, he just keeps getting up and moving forward... with patience and wisdom, and courage and grace.

Michelle Obama

Success means having the courage, the determination, and the will to become the person you believe you were meant to be.

George A. Sheehan

If one suffers we all suffer. Togetherness is strength. Courage.

Jean-Bertrand Aristide

Optimism is the foundation of courage.

Nicholas M. Butler

Washington's answer to a self-inflicted financial crisis reminded Americans why they so deeply distrust the political class. The 'fiscal cliff' process was secretive and sloppy, and the nation's so-called leadership lacked the political courage to address our root problems: joblessness and debt.

Ron Fournier

Often the difference between a successful man and a failure is not one's better abilities or ideas, but the courage that one has to bet on his ideas, to take a calculated risk, and to act.

Maxwell Maltz

There has to be this pioneer, the individual who has the courage, the ambition to overcome the obstacles that always develop when one tries to do something worthwhile, especially when it is new and different.

Alfred P. Sloan

Our situation today shows that beauty demands for itself at least as much courage and decision as do truth and goodness, and she will not allow herself to be separated and banned from her two sisters without taking them along with herself in an act of mysterious vengeance.

Hans Urs von Balthasar

True courage is like a kite; a contrary wind raises it higher.

John Petit-Senn

There never is a good time for tough decisions. There will always be an election or something else. You have to pick courage and do it. Governance is about taking tough, even unpopular, decisions.

Jairam Ramesh

In the central place of every heart, there is a recording chamber; so long as it receives messages of beauty, hope, cheer and courage, you are young.

Samuel Ullman

Is he alone who has courage on his right hand and faith on his left hand?

Charles Lindbergh

Success is that old ABC - ability, breaks, and courage.

Charles Luckman

Killing yourself is a major commitment, it takes a kind of

courage. Most people just lead lives of cowardly desperation. It's kinda half suicide where you just dull yourself with substances.

Robert Crumb

Support the strong, give courage to the timid, remind the indifferent, and warn the opposed.

Whitney M. Young

He who has faith has... an inward reservoir of courage, hope, confidence, calmness, and assuring trust that all will come out well - even though to the world it may appear to come out most badly.

B. C. Forbes

Courage and willingness to just go for it, whether it is a conversation or a spontaneous trip or trying new things that are scary - it is a really attractive quality.

Alanis Morissette

If the Christian is a restorationist, a legalist, if he wants everything clear and safe, then he will find nothing.

Tradition and memory of the past must help us to have the courage to open up new areas to God.

Pope Francis

If you want to lose 40 pounds, you order salad instead of fries. If you want to be a better friend, you take the phone call instead of screening it. If you want to write a novel, you sit down and write a single paragraph. It's scary to make major changes, but we usually have enough courage to take the next right step.

Regina Brett

We all know the dangers of sequels. Lightning doesn't strike twice in the same place too often, and I think you've got to move beyond it, go the extra mile and have the courage not to just repeat the first one.

Colin Firth

I've been through it all, baby, I'm mother courage.

Elizabeth Taylor

Guilt is just as powerful, but its influence is positive, while shame's is destructive. Shame erodes our courage and fuels disengagement.

Brene Brown

Nothing gives a fearful man more courage than another's fear.

Umberto Eco

We learned to be patient observers like the owl. We learned cleverness from the crow, and courage from the jay, who will attack an owl ten times its size to drive it off its territory. But above all of them ranked the chickadee because of its indomitable spirit.

Tom Brown, Jr.

It takes courage to sit on a jury. How many of us want to decide the fate of another person's life or freedom? How many of us want to hold that kind of power in our hands?

Regina Brett

The criteria for serving one's country should be competence, courage and willingness to serve. When we deny people the chance to serve because of their sexual orientation, we deprive them of their rights of citizenship, and we deprive our armed forces the service of willing and capable Americans.

Dianne Feinstein

He's a man of great common sense and good taste - meaning thereby a man without originality or moral courage.

George Bernard Shaw

Each person has inside a basic decency and goodness. If he listens to it and acts on it, he is giving a great deal of what it is the world needs most. It is not complicated but it takes courage. It takes courage for a person to listen to his own goodness and act on it.

Pablo Casals

Often the difference between a successful person and a failure is not one has better abilities or ideas, but the courage that one has to bet on one's ideas, to take a calculated risk - and to act.

Andre Malraux

My mother taught me that we all have the power to achieve our dreams. What I lacked was the courage.

Clay Aiken

But courage which goes against military expediency is stupidity, or, if it is insisted upon by a commander, irresponsibility.

Erwin Rommel

Anyone can support a team that is winning - it takes no courage. But to stand behind a team to defend a team when it is down and really needs you, that takes a lot of courage.

Bart Starr

We've let the blade of our innocence dull over time, and it's only in innocence that you find any kind of magic, any kind of courage.

Sean Penn

I admire the courage and self-reliance it takes to start your own business and make it succeed.

Martha Stewart

Curiosity, rationalization, and laziness are no match against courage, self-control, and mental toughness.

John Bytheway

I have spent a great deal of my life being part of minorities. Some of the people I admire the most in the world have had the courage to defend, against wind and tide, minority viewpoints in those frightening times when any disagreement with universal conformity is identified as treason.

Antonio Munoz Molina

Courage is a mean with regard to fear and confidence.

Aristotle

Just as courage imperils life, fear protects it.

Leonardo da Vinci

Untutored courage is useless in the face of educated bullets.

George S. Patton

All of us have moments in our lives that test our courage. Taking children into a house with a white carpet is one of them.

Erma Bombeck

A mode of conduct, a standard of courage, discipline, fortitude and integrity can do a great deal to make a woman beautiful.

Jacqueline Bisset

To persevere, trusting in what hopes he has, is courage in a man.

Euripides

Courage stands halfway between cowardice and rashness, one of which is a lack, the other an excess of courage.

Plutarch

Religion in its humility restores man to his only dignity, the courage to live by grace.

George Santayana

This soul, or life within us, by no means agrees with the life outside us. If one has the courage to ask her what she thinks, she is always saying the very opposite to what other people say.

Virginia Woolf

Then there is a still higher type of courage - the courage to brave pain, to live with it, to never let others know of it and to still find joy in life; to wake up in the morning with an enthusiasm for the day ahead.

Howard Cosell

Determination, energy, and courage appear spontaneously when we care deeply about something. We take risks that are unimaginable in any other context.

Margaret J. Wheatley

Let a new earth rise. Let another world be born. Let a bloody peace be written in the sky. Let a second generation full of courage issue forth; let a people loving freedom come to growth.

Margaret Walker

It takes vision and courage to create - it takes faith and courage to prove.

Owen D. Young

Courage is a special kind of knowledge: the knowledge of how to fear what ought to be feared and how not to fear what ought not to be feared.

David Ben-Gurion

Men have a psychological need to show off their courage and strength. When he sees you talking to another guy, that instinct kicks in and he jumps to protect you and prove he's worthy of your love.

Helen Fisher

I have the responsibility of over four million people, and I am in a position to do good, to be able to bring about a new life for my people, and I will continue to move in that direction. It's a burden, but it needs to be done, and you have to have the courage and wisdom to see it through.

Abdallah II of Jordan

Alas, nothing reveals man the way war does. Nothing so accentuates in him the beauty and ugliness, the intelligence and foolishness, the brutishness and humanity, the courage and cowardice, the enigma.

Oriana Fallaci

Courage is very important. Like a muscle, it is strengthened by use.

Ruth Gordon

The only thing is, people have to develop courage. It is most important of all the virtues. Because without courage, you can't practice any other virtues consistently.

Maya Angelou

Just as courage is the danger of life, so is fear its safeguard.

Leonardo da Vinci

Every day begins with an act of courage and hope: getting out of bed.

Mason Cooley

Courage consists not in hazarding without fear; but being resolutely minded in a just cause.

Plutarch

For thousands of years, human beings have been obsessed with beauty, truth, love, honor, altruism, courage, social relationships, art, and God. They all go together as subjective experiences, and it's a straw man to set God up as the delusion. If he is, then so is truth itself or beauty itself.

Deepak Chopra

Audacity augments courage; hesitation, fear.

Publilius Syrus

I'm sick of not having the courage to be an absolute nobody.

J. D. Salinger

The best marriages are the ones where we can go out in the world and really put ourselves out there. A lot of times we'll fail, and sometimes we'll pull it off. But good marriages are when you can go home and know that your vulnerability will be honored as courage, and that you'll find support.

Brene Brown

I have the courage of my convictions.

Brigitte Bardot

The gospel alone liberates you to live a life of scandalous generosity, unrestrained sacrifice, uncommon valor, and unbounded courage.

Tullian Tchividjian

There are two types of courage involved with what I did. When it comes to picking up a rifle, millions of people are capable of doing that, as we see in Iraq or Vietnam. But when it comes to risking their careers, or risking being invited to lunch by the establishment, it turns out that's remarkably rare.

Daniel Ellsberg

At my aunt's funeral, I promised myself that I wouldn't be
bound by the belief that I'm supposed to stay in anything -
whether it's a relationship, a job, a house, or a circumstance
- if it makes me miserable. She gave me the courage to find
my own happiness.

Jill Scott

What has made America amazing has been the fact that
throughout our history, throughout the more than 200 years
of our history, there have been men and women of courage
who stood up and decided it was more important to look
out for the future of their children and their grandchildren
than their own political futures.

Scott Walker

Your determination, selflessness and courage have brought
the freedom struggle towards its fulfilment.

Gerry Adams

I can tell you character traits I admire and work to develop in myself - perseverance, self-discipline, courage to stand up for what is right even when it is against one's friends or one's self.

Dalia Mogahed

Ingenuity, plus courage, plus work, equals miracles.

Bob Richards

Had we lived I should have had a tale to tell of the hardihood, endurance and courage of my companions which would have stirred the heart of every Englishman. These rough notes and our dead bodies must tell the tale.

Robert Falcon Scott

Moral courage is higher and a rarer virtue than physical courage.

William Slim

The man who has the courage of his platitudes is always a successful man.

Van Wyck Brooks

Courage - you develop courage by doing small things like just as if you wouldn't want to pick up a 100-pound weight without preparing yourself.

Maya Angelou

Believers, look up - take courage. The angels are nearer than you think.

Billy Graham

Real nobility is based on scorn, courage, and profound indifference.

Albert Camus

Every human being on this earth is born with a tragedy, and it isn't original sin. He's born with the tragedy that he has to grow up... a lot of people don't have the courage to do it.

Helen Hayes

We need to find the courage to say no to the things and people that are not serving us if we want to rediscover ourselves and live our lives with authenticity.

Barbara de Angelis

Peace comes when you talk to the guy you most hate. And that's where the courage of a leader comes, because when you sit down with your enemy, you as a leader must already have very considerable confidence from your own constituency.

Desmond Tutu

It is a blessed thing that in every age some one has had the individuality enough and courage enough to stand by his own convictions.

Robert Green Ingersoll

When God speaks, oftentimes His voice will call for an act of courage on our part.

Charles Stanley

Some people have a hard time getting rid of stuff. If that's you, pray for God to give you the courage to get rid of things you don't really need or things He wants you to give away. This will help keep your surroundings organized and clutter-free.

Joyce Meyer

People think I have courage. The courage in my family are
my wife Pam, my three daughters, here, Nicole, Jamie,
LeeAnn, my mom, who's right here too.

Jim Valvano

To dare to live alone is the rarest courage; since there are
many who had rather meet their bitterest enemy in the field,
than their own hearts in their closet.

Charles Caleb Colton

Courage can't see around corners but goes around them
anyway.

Mignon McLaughlin

Without courage, wisdom bears no fruit.

Baltasar Gracian

Courage and grace are a formidable mixture. The only
place to see it is in the bullring.

Marlene Dietrich

It takes as much courage to have tried and failed as it does to have tried and succeeded.

Anne Morrow Lindbergh

There are pretenders to piety as well as to courage.

Moliere

Those who won our independence... valued liberty as an end and as a means. They believed liberty to be the secret of happiness and courage to be the secret of liberty.

Louis D. Brandeis

Courage that grows from constitution often forsakes a man when he has occasion for it; courage which arises from a sense of duty acts; in a uniform manner.

Joseph Addison

In fact, my courage and my bravery at a young age was the thing I was bullied for, a kind of 'Who do you think you are?'

Lady Gaga

Courage consists not in blindly overlooking danger, but in seeing it, and conquering it.

Jean Paul

The one man other than my father who made the most lasting impression was an uncle, Serge B. Benson. He taught me in three different classes - but above all, he taught me lessons in moral, physical, and intellectual courage that I have tried to apply in later life.

Ezra Taft Benson

We are biological creatures. We are born, we live, we die. There is no transcendent purpose to existence. At best we are creatures of reason, and by using reason we can cure ourselves of emotional excess. Purged of both hope and fear, we find courage in the face of helplessness, insignificance and uncertainty.

Jonathan Sacks

Discouragement is not the absence of adequacy but the absence of courage.

Neal A. Maxwell

I think there's a difference between ditzy and dumb. Dumb is just not knowing. Ditzy is having the courage to ask!

Jessica Simpson

Rather like Batman, I embody the themes of the movie which are the values of family, courage and compassion and a sense of right and wrong, good and bad and justice.

Gary Oldman

When you have a wife who has been a tower of strength and shown more courage than you dreamed existed - that's the finest I know.

Lou Gehrig

As a shame researcher, I know that the very best thing to do in the midst of a shame attack is totally counterintuitive: Practice courage and reach out!

Brene Brown

Men create real miracles when they use their God-given courage and intelligence.

Jean Anouilh

While President Bush likes to project an image of strength and courage, the real truth is that in the presence of his large financial contributors, he is a moral coward.

Al Gore

I look back at the looks I've had over the years. I'm proud of myself that I had the courage to experiment with crazy hairstyles and some fashion things. Would I do it again? No. But that's part of the learning process and getting from point A to point B.

Christina Aguilera

In times of conflict, war, poverty or religious fundamentalism, women and children are the first and most numerous victims. Women need all their courage today.

Isabel Allende

The valor and courage of our young women and men in the armed services are a shining example to all of the world, and we owe them and their families our deepest respect.

Bill Frist

Love is the most difficult and dangerous form of courage. Courage is the most desperate, admirable and noble kind of love.

Delmore Schwartz

It's not just Bin Laden or just those that are involved in the counterterrorism effort. We've gotta cast the net broader than that. But I think it's a - very special tribute that we all owe to the bravery and courage of the men and women in the intelligence and military business who performed so well to finally get it done.

Dick Cheney

Most of man's problems upon this planet, in the long history of the race, have been met and solved either partially or as a whole by experiment based on common sense and carried out with courage.

Frances Perkins

The enchanting charms of this sublime science reveal only to those who have the courage to go deeply into it.

Carl Friedrich Gauss

With courage and character, American soldiers continue to put themselves on the line to defend our freedom, and so many have paid the ultimate sacrifice.

Dan Lipinski

Rosa Parks' courage, determination, and tenacity continue to be an inspiration to all those committed to non-violent protest and change nearly half a century later.

Bob Filner

I think we spend so much of our lives trying to pretend that we know what's going to happen next. In fact we don't. To recognize that we don't know even what will happen this afternoon and yet having the courage to move forward - that's one meaning of faith.

Sharon Salzberg

Women's courage is rather different from men's. The fact that women have to bring up children and look after husbands makes them braver at facing long-term issues, such as illness. Men are more immediately courageous. Lots of people are brave in battle.

Mary Wesley

I have always had the courage for the new things that life sometimes offers.

Wallis Simpson

It is right to endure with resignation what the gods send, and to face one's enemies with courage.

Pericles

When our mothers are alive and healthy, they do extraordinary things... like the mothers of Plaza de Mayo, who marched in Argentinean plazas, defying the military junta dictatorship and demanding the whereabouts of their abducted children... or the Liberian mothers who faced down civil war armed only with T-shirts and courage.

Liya Kebede

Next to courage, willpower is the most important thing in politics.

Paul Johnson

Part of courage is simple consistency.

Peggy Noonan

The courage of a soldier is heightened by his knowledge of his profession.

Publius Flavius Vegetius Renatus

A life lesson for me is, how do you muster the courage to take on a new risk? Whether it's starting up a business or taking on a new project or expedition. I think the risks that we take are all relative to the risk-taker.

Ann Bancroft

Men was formed for society, and is neither capable of living alone, nor has the courage to do it.

William Blackstone

People shouldn't look at me and think life is one big piece of glamour. That's the marketing, the spin. Life is challenging. But I have courage, strength, and enough good health to see the positive.

Carmen Dell'Orefice

No man in the world has more courage than the man who can stop after eating one peanut.

Channing Pollock

Elizabeth Keckley was a woman of remarkable strength, courage, perseverance, and dignity. She was exceptionally talented, but also very diligent and ambitious, and together those qualities enabled her to deliver herself from slavery and become a successful businesswoman.

Jennifer Chiaverini

I would kiss you, had I the courage.

Edouard Manet

In 'Tree of Life,' the cinematography records a small story, a celebration of the courage of everyday life. But it does it so up close and so effortlessly that it has the effect of elevating the intimacy of the story to a grand scale.

Caleb Deschanel

Design is the courage and brilliance to cover an original and make it different.

John Hockenberry

A nation which has forgotten the quality of courage which in the past has been brought to public life is not as likely to insist upon or regard that quality in its chosen leaders today - and in fact we have forgotten.

John F. Kennedy

A man of great common sense and good taste - meaning thereby a man without originality or moral courage.

George Bernard Shaw

I never thought much of the courage of a lion tamer. Inside the cage he is at least safe from people.

George Bernard Shaw

Keep your fears to yourself, but share your courage with others.

Robert Louis Stevenson

Give us grace and strength to forbear and to persevere. Give us courage and gaiety and the quiet mind, spare to us our friends, soften to us our enemies.

Robert Louis Stevenson

Sometimes even to live is an act of courage.

Lucius Annaeus Seneca

There is nothing in the world so much admired as a man who knows how to bear unhappiness with courage.

Lucius Annaeus Seneca

I have a hat. It is graceful and feminine and give me a certain dignity, as if I were attending a state funeral or something. Someday I may get up enough courage to wear it, instead of carrying it.

Erma Bombeck

Women have to summon up courage to fulfill dormant dreams.

Alice Walker

Courage is almost a contradiction in terms. It means a strong desire to live taking the form of readiness to die.

Gilbert K. Chesterton

Many a man will have the courage to die gallantly, but will not have the courage to say, or even to think, that the cause for which he is asked to die is an unworthy one.

Bertrand Russell

The paradox of courage is that a man must be a little careless of his life even in order to keep it.

Gilbert K. Chesterton

The weak in courage is strong in cunning.

William Blake

Unless a reviewer has the courage to give you unqualified praise, I say ignore the bastard.

John Steinbeck

It takes someone with a vision of the possibilities to attain new levels of experience. Someone with the courage to live his dreams.

Les Brown

You have to have courage to be obedient to God.

Charles Stanley

The courage to be is rooted in the God who appears when God has disappeared in the anxiety of doubt.

Paul Tillich

Suffering! We owe to it all that is good in us, all that gives value to life; we owe to it pity, we owe to it courage, we owe to it all the virtues.

Anatole France

Perfect courage is to do without witnesses what one would be capable of doing with the world looking on.

Francois de La Rochefoucauld

You will find as you grow older that courage is the rarest of all qualities to be found in public life.

Benjamin Disraeli

Courage without conscience is a wild beast.

Robert Green Ingersoll

If human beings had genuine courage, they'd wear their costumes every day of the year, not just on Halloween.

Douglas Coupland

The courage of the poet is to keep ajar the door that leads into madness.

Christopher Morley

Traits like humility, courage, and empathy are easily overlooked - but it's immensely important to find them in your closest relationships.

Laura Linney

There can be no great courage where there is no confidence or assurance, and half the battle is in the conviction that we can do what we undertake.

Orison Swett Marden

Eccentricity has always abounded when and where strength of character had abounded; and the amount of eccentricity in a society has generally been proportional to the amount of genius, mental vigor, and courage which it contained.

John Stuart Mill

Despair gives courage to a coward.

Thomas Fuller

The strangest, most generous, and proudest of all virtues is true courage.

Michel de Montaigne

The psychologist Elizabeth Loftus has shown great courage, in the face of spiteful vested interests, in demonstrating how easy it is for people to concoct memories that are entirely false but which seem, to the victim, every bit as real as true memories.

Richard Dawkins

Way down deep, we're all motivated by the same urges. Cats have the courage to live by them.

Jim Davis

Courage enlarges, cowardice diminishes resources. In desperate straits the fears of the timid aggravate the dangers that imperil the brave.

Christian Nestell Bovee

We are very much what others think of us. The reception our observations meet with gives us courage to proceed, or damps our efforts.

William Hazlitt

Courage is simply the willingness to be afraid and act anyway.

Robert Anthony

It takes a lot of courage to face up to things you can't do because we feed ourselves so much denial.

Zoe Saldana

Great tragedy has come to us, and we are meeting it with the best that is in our country, with courage and concern for others because this is America. This is who we are.

George W. Bush

In strife who inquires whether stratagem or courage was used?

Virgil

Courage is what preserves our liberty, safety, life, and our homes and parents, our country and children. Courage comprises all things.

Plautus

Whether you be man or woman you will never do anything in this world without courage. It is the greatest quality of the mind next to honor.

James Allen

There are always a few who stand up in times of communal madness and have the courage to say that what unites us is greater than what divides us.

Geraldine Brooks

Courage easily finds its own eloquence.

Plautus

If we can understand that death is not the end but is really a transition into the next life, the great part of life, that frees us up into receiving God's courage and his help.

Max Lucado

Courage conquers all things: it even gives strength to the

body.

Ovid

You cannot build character and courage by destroying men's initiative and independence.

William J. H. Boetcker

Good courage in a bad affair is half of the evil overcome.

Plautus

Patience, that blending of moral courage with physical timidity.

Thomas Hardy

Muslims must speak out and explain who they are, what they believe in, what they stand for, what is the meaning of their life. They must have the courage to denounce what is said and done by certain Muslims in the name of their religion.

Tariq Ramadan

Falsehood is cowardice, the truth courage.

Hosea Ballou

If we are to survive, we must have ideas, vision, and courage. These things are rarely produced by committees. Everything that matters in our intellectual and moral life begins with an individual confronting his own mind and conscience in a room by himself.

Arthur M. Schlesinger, Jr.

At the bottom of not a little of the bravery that appears in the world, there lurks a miserable cowardice. Men will face powder and steel because they have not the courage to face public opinion.

Edwin Hubbel Chapin

With compassion you can die for other people, like the mother who can die for her child. You have the courage to say it because you are not afraid of losing anything, because you know that understanding and love is the foundation of happiness. But if you have fear of losing your status, your position, you will not have the courage to do it.

Thich Nhat Hanh

I have reached the conclusion that those who have physical courage also have moral courage. Physical courage is a great test.

Oriana Fallaci

I don't understand why people say that I am full of courage. I feel terribly nervous.

Aung San Suu Kyi

Courage is the art of being the only one who knows you're scared to death.

Earl Wilson

What we want from modern dance is courage and audacity.

Twyla Tharp

A man of courage never needs weapons, but he may need bail.

Lewis Mumford

The courage of a soldier is found to be the cheapest and most common quality of human nature.

Edward Gibbon

The last thing a woman will consent to discover in a man whom she loves, or on whom she simply depends, is want of courage.

Joseph Conrad

I was a little doubtful about the propriety of going to the Mammoth Cave without a gentleman escort, but if two ladies travel alone they must have the courage of men.

Maria Mitchell

Nothing gives us courage more readily than the desire to avoid looking like a damn fool.

Dean Koontz

We're going to be OK because of the American people. They have more grit, determination and courage than you can imagine.

Joe Biden

Courage is managing fear to accomplish what you want to accomplish. And it's a great demonstration of love. It's really what love is. It's finding areas in which other people are more important than you.

Rudy Giuliani

Conscience is the root of all true courage; if a man would be brave let him obey his conscience.

James Freeman Clarke

Leadership requires the courage to make decisions that will benefit the next generation.

Alan Autry

Lying at the root of the social agreements of 1980 are the courage, sense of responsibility, and the solidarity of the working people. Both sides have then recognized that an accord must be reached if bloodshed is to be prevented.

Lech Walesa

Grave was the man in years, in looks, in word, his locks were grey, yet was his courage green.

Torquato Tasso

Americans are gathering the courage to just say no. We are saying no to addictive consumer lifestyles. We are saying no to wars and corporate takeover and the IMF loans that gobble up people and their resources.

Cynthia McKinney

Courage is willingness to take the risk once you know the odds. Optimistic overconfidence means you are taking the risk because you don't know the odds. It's a big difference.

Daniel Kahneman

To me, there is no greater act of courage than being the one who kisses first.

Janeane Garofalo

Have the courage of your desire.

George Gissing

Often the test of courage is not to die but to live.

Vittorio Alfieri

I realize now that I've hoped to be great - as an actress, as a mother - because I want to embody the greatness of women who didn't get to be all they could have been. Their dignity, their courage, and their brilliance make me strive to be better. They're a part of me.

Salma Hayek

We had no more courage than Harriet Tubman or Marcus Garvey had in their times. We just had a more vulnerable enemy.

Stokely Carmichael

I always disliked dogs, those protectors of cowards who lack the courage to fight an assailant themselves.

August Strindberg

It takes a good deal of physical courage to ride a horse. This, however, I have. I get it at about forty cents a flask, and take it as required.

Stephen Leacock

It would be sad if we lost our instinct and our courage to love and protect.

Emeli Sande

For this equilibrium now in sight, let us trust that mankind, as it has occurred in the greatest periods of its past, will find for itself a new code of ethics, common to all, made of tolerance, of courage, and of faith in the Spirit of men.

Albert Claude

Courage is poorly housed that dwells in numbers; the lion never counts the herd that are about him, nor weighs how many flocks he has to scatter.

Aaron Hill

Some of the greatest survivors have been women. Look at the courage so many women have shown after surviving earthquakes in the rubble for days on end.

Bear Grylls

It is easy enough to praise men for the courage of their convictions. I wish I could teach the sad young of this mealy generation the courage of their confusions.

John Ciardi

Students teach all sorts of things but most importantly they make explicit the courage that it takes to be a learner, the courage it takes to open yourself to the transformative power of real learning and that courage I am exposed to almost every day at MIT and that I'm deeply grateful for.

Junot Diaz

I have a lot of courage. I'm a realist.

Elisabeth Rohm

To bathe a cat takes brute force, perseverance, courage of conviction - and a cat. The last ingredient is usually hardest to come by.

Stephen Baker

Remarkable contributions are typically spawned by a

passionate commitment to transcendent values such as beauty, truth, wisdom, justice, charity, fidelity, joy, courage and honor.

Gary Hamel

Overcoming the Cold War required courage from the people of Central and Eastern Europe and what was then the German Democratic Republic, but it also required the steadfastness of Western partner over many decades when many had long lost hope of integration of the two Germanys and Europe.

Angela Merkel

We are telling the American people to have patience, courage, resolve and determination.

Muammar al-Gaddafi

A military coup needs a sacrifice and courage that you can't find in an army without morale.

Jalal Talabani

None speak of the bravery, the might, or the intellect of

Jesus; but the devil is always imagined as a being of acute intellect, political cunning, and the fiercest courage. These universal and instinctive tendencies of the human mind reveal much.

Lydia M. Child

Have the courage to be ignorant of a great number of things, in order to avoid the calamity of being ignorant of everything.

Sydney Smith

Whether you be man or woman you will never do anything in this world without courage. It is the greatest quality of the mind next to honor.

James Lane Allen

The word 'courage,' one of my favorite words, the root or the etymology of that word is 'cour,' which means heart. I think true courage is actually following your heart and not getting or succumbing to what other people's definition of what your life should be. Live your life.

Hill Harper

The courage in journalism is sticking up for the unpopular, not the popular.

Geraldo Rivera

Courage is... the knowledge of how to fear what ought to be feared and how not to fear what ought not to be feared.

David Ben-Gurion

Only choices made in love are compassionate. There are no exceptions. Do you have the courage to act with an empowered heart without attachment to the outcome? If not, you have no ability to give or experience compassion. That is the shocking truth.

Gary Zukav

There is not a single Muslim leader today who has the courage and commitment to defend Islam and Muslims, they are all in awe of the United States and other Western powers, and are indebted to them.

Abu Bakar Bashir

I went through a long period where I was afraid of doing

things I wanted to do, and you get your courage back, which is what's important.

George Michael

On sensitive issues, talk isn't cheap - it takes real courage to pry open topics nailed shut.

Marvin Olasky

Pugnacity is a form of courage, but a very bad form.

Sinclair Lewis

Limit to courage? There is no limit to courage.

Gabriele D'Annunzio

When you really believe in God, it gives you a courage, a confidence that enables you to meet the things coming.

Della Reese

Whatever the long-term legal prospects for same-sex marriage, President Obama's willingness to put the matter front and center in an election year can at least make him a candidate for inclusion in Kennedy's Profiles in Courage.

Robert Dallek

I think that the romantic impulse is in all of us and that sometimes we live it for a short time, but it's not part of a sensible way of living. It's a heroic path and it generally ends dangerously. I treasure it in the sense that I believe it's a path of great courage. It can also be the path of the foolhardy and the compulsive.

Jane Campion

Parents do not have the courage to say no to certain things that their children demand. They are rather scared of their children.

Shiv Khera

For a long time, it was like I was part of some special forces unit: I'd land, meet everyone, five minutes later I'd have to do some amazing work, then - boom! - I'm out again. You know, playing supporting parts takes courage.

John C. Reilly

To go to hospitals and see people fight and overcome cystic fibrosis or cancer or any number of illnesses is to see courage that is humbling. And athletes constantly need to be humbled.

Dale Murphy

Being gifted needs courage.

Georg Brandes

You take a number of small steps which you believe are right, thinking maybe tomorrow somebody will treat this as a dangerous provocation. And then you wait. If there is no reaction, you take another step: courage is only an accumulation of small steps.

George Konrad

Courage is the fear of being thought a coward.

Horace Smith

Courage is always the surest wisdom.

Wilfred Grenfell

In all the difficult decisions that I made through the course of running Loudcloud and Opsware, I never once felt brave. In fact, I often felt scared to death. I never lost those feelings, but after much practice, I learned to ignore them. That learning process might also be called the courage development process.

Ben Horowitz

It takes great courage to be vulnerable. It takes enormous strength to be a real woman.

John Eldredge

I'm not a fighter, but I would love to be a boxer because I love the courage and toughness. I mean, there can be nothing more terrifying than walking into an arena and looking at Mike Tyson in the ring.

Mark McGrath

Success, they taught me, is built on the foundation of courage, hard-work and individual responsibility. Despite what some would have us believe, success is not built on resentment and fears.

Susana Martinez

The older people that one admires seem to be fearless. They go right out into the world. It's astounding. Maybe they can't see or they can't hear, but they walk out into the street and take life as it comes. They're models of courage, in a strange way.

James Hillman

Being tall has a major impact in general. It takes some courage to be as big as you are - to live up to it and not be intimidated by the graceful tiny people.

Sigourney Weaver

Well, I think that - I think leadership's always been about two main things: imagination and courage.

Paul Keating

In the military, you learn the essence of people. You see so many examples of self-sacrifice and moral courage. In the rest of life, you don't get that many opportunities to be sure of your friends.

Adam Driver

I love revolutionaries who have the courage to stand up against the status quo. They're always misunderstood, but they're the ones who are standing up for human rights.

Richard Hatch

It takes both courage and talent to stand up in front of fellow human beings and make them crack a smile, and at the same time keep it clean.

Ray Comfort

One has to have the courage of one's pessimism.

Ian Mcewan

There were times when chemo would eat my body, but I told myself that I have the strength and courage to win and come out stronger.

Yuvraj Singh

It is a wise man who knows where courage ends and

stupidity begins.

Jerome Cady

When we have done our best, we can, as a united people, take whatever may befall with calm courage and confidence that this old nation will survive and if death should come to many of us, death is not the end.

Eamon de Valera

To be a Bond girl you need courage, charm, determination and feistiness.

Olga Kurylenko

With his trademark courage and conviction, President Reagan led us out of the Cold War, spreading his vision of freedom, resulting in the release of millions of people from the yoke of communism.

John Doolittle

Buddhist practices offer a way of saying, 'Hey, come back over here, reconnect.' The only way that you'll actually wake up and have some freedom is if you have the capacity and courage to stay with the vulnerability and the discomfort.

Tara Brach

Maybe you will be afraid and maybe you will fail, but the courage to take risks in any part of your life is, I feel, a very worthwhile way to live.

Emile Hirsch

I have huge respect for women who go out of their homes and have the courage to make their own destiny. And let me tell you, Indian women are doing a great job. There are those who work because they have no option but to earn, and then there are those who do it because they have the right talent. I respect both.

Shilpa Shetty

I think there's a growing courage among the younger generation of American writers. Because of the more superficial treatment of characters taking place in cinema, they have had to deal with that by digging deeper into who these people are.

Mohsin Hamid

Make-up is the last thing to enhance your beauty, but it's very important because it builds up your self-confidence and gives you more courage.

Evelyn Lauder

Greatness, in the last analysis, is largely bravery - courage in escaping from old ideas and old standards and respectable ways of doing things.

James Harvey Robinson

With faith and courage, generations of Armenians have overcome great suffering and proudly preserved their culture, traditions, and religion and have told the story of the genocide to an often indifferent world.

Jerry Costello

War paralyzes your courage and deadens the spirit of true manhood.

Alexander Berkman

More firm and sure the hand of courage strikes, when it

obeys the watchful eye of caution.

James Thomson

Throughout the years, many Christian women have told me of their great respect for the bravery and courage evident in my work, perhaps even gesturing to their own Isis earrings or a Nile River Goddess pendants.

Carol P. Christ

When we read stories of heroes, we identify with them. We take the journey with them. We see how the obstacles almost overcome them. We see how they grow as human beings or gain qualities or show great qualities of strength and courage and with them, we grow in some small way.

Sam Raimi

The problem is when you are writing something in retrospective, it needs a lot of courage not to change, or you will forget a certain reality, and you will just take in consideration your view today.

Boutros Boutros-Ghali

Freedom. And Justice. If you have those two, it covers everything. You must stick to those principles and have the courage of your convictions.

Ian Smith

Our film examines the heroism, courage and prowess of the Soviet submarine force in ways never seen before.

Kathryn Bigelow

Therefore, don't let sinners take courage to think they will be favoured like the thief on the cross; for we see on the other side, they may be like the hardened one, and reproach death itself.

Elias Hicks

I believe that art has been a vehicle for me that's been about enlightenment and expanding my own parameters, to give me courage to exercise the freedom that I have in life.

Jeff Koons

If nothing else, I want women to understand that they are powerful. If you look back at history, in almost every big moment, in every leap forward, you find ordinary women at the core. We have more ability to make changes in the world than we can imagine if we have the courage to try.

Liya Kebede

Let who will boast their courage in the field, I find but little safety from my shield, Nature's, not honour's law we must obey: This made me cast my useless shield away.

Archilochus

To show the world what long experience gains, requires not courage, though it calls for pains; but at life's outset to inform mankind is a bold effort of a valiant mind.

George Crabbe

I really thank my parents for giving me the good sense to not get into anything wrong. There are many people around who like controversies, and I actually wonder how do they do it. I don't have the courage to get into controversies. There are people who love it; I find it silly.

Saina Nehwal

I think laughter may be a form of courage. As humans we sometimes stand tall and look into the sun and laugh, and I think we are never more brave than when we do that.

Linda Ellerbee

Remember that when you meet your antagonist, to do everything in a mild agreeable manner. Let your courage be keen, but, at the same time, as polished as your sword.

Richard Brinsley Sheridan

My definition of courage is never letting anyone define you.

Jenna Jameson

There is a measure needing courage to adopt and enforce it, which I believe to be of virtue sufficient to redeem the nation in this its darkest hour: one only; I know of no other to which we may rationally trust for relief from impending dangers without and within.

Robert Dale Owen

The true legacy of 9-11 cannot be found among political

leaders of the day, but in the citizen soldiers and public safety personnel who answered that day with courage and selflessness.

Mike Pence

Even in the hardest circumstances, dreams can give you the courage to live, and I hope I can share that message with children in need.

Yuna Kim

Although the war in which you fought took place more than half-a-century ago, your courage, your sacrifice and your patriotism reaches through the decades and inspires us today.

Mike Ferguson

These rules may seem simple enough, but it will require great morale and physical courage to adhere to them. But if carried out in the strict sense of the word it will surely lead to a greater success than could otherwise be attained.

Major Taylor

I would love to be a Franciscan brother. I'm just not sure I have the courage to do it.

Rich Mullins

During the long process of history, by relying on our own diligence, courage and wisdom, Chinese people have opened up a good and beautiful home where all ethnic groups live in harmony and fostered an excellent culture that never fades.

Xi Jinping

With honesty of purpose, balance, a respect for tradition, courage, and, above all, a philosophy of life, any young person who embraces the historical profession will find it rich in rewards and durable in satisfaction.

Samuel E. Morison

To him that waits all things reveal themselves, provided that he has the courage not to deny, in the darkness, what he has seen in the light.

Coventry Patmore

I have written a memoir here and there, and that takes its own form of selfishness and courage. However, generally speaking, I have no interest in writing about my own life or intruding in the privacy of those around me.

Peter Carey

It is remarkable that this people, though unarmed, dares attack an armed foe; the infantry defy the cavalry, and by their activity and courage generally prove victors.

Giraldus Cambrensis

Our young people have come to look upon war as a kind of beneficent deity, which not only adds to the national honor but uplifts a nation and develops patriotism and courage.

Rebecca Harding Davis

What I love about the East End is that there's a great perseverance, determination and courage. What I dislike about it is that there is sometimes a celebration of ignorance.

Eddie Marsan

For the past 25 years as an adoption attorney, I have witnessed the extraordinary courage and compassion of women - from age 14 to 40 - facing unplanned pregnancy. Not once did I believe that the government should interfere with their personal and private decision.

Ann McLane Kuster

I like Beryl Bainbridge a great deal, and she is a writer who absolutely demands to be read a second, third, and fourth time. I admire her great courage in leaving so much unsaid and asking the reader to really engage her brain.

Monica Ali

I pray they will carry on in spite of that dreadful monster prejudice, and with patience, courage, fortitude and perseverance achieve success for themselves.

Major Taylor

I'm an exile. My father had the courage to leave with his wife, his mother and three children under twelve. It took more courage to leave, to sacrifice everything for freedom, than to stay.

Andy Garcia

It is our conduct, our patriotism and belief in our American way of life, our courage that will win the final battle.

Prescott Bush

As the first Hispanic female governor in history, little girls often come up to me in the grocery store or the mall. They look and point, and when they get the courage, they ask 'Are you Susana?' and they run up and give me a hug.

Susana Martinez

True courage is a result of reasoning. A brave mind is always impregnable.

Jeremy Collier

Whatever enlarges hope will also exalt courage.

William Samuel Johnson

Ronald Reagan's well documented final battles with Alzheimer's disease were fought with the same conviction and courage that his many public battles were fought.

William L. Jenkins

When who you are naturally is not only considered a sin, but you're reviled for being that human being and you don't have any control over it, there are lots of issues that come into play. And it takes a lot of presence, determination, courage and space to figure out how to land in that truth regardless of what anyone around you thinks about it.

Billy Porter

In our film profession you may have Gable's looks, Tracy's art, Marlene's legs or Liz's violet eyes, but they don't mean a thing without that swinging thing called courage.

Frank Capra

Unfortunately, unless we're focused on building up our courage, which gives us our self-confidence and all that we need to make quantum change in our lives, the voice of fear will always take the lead inside our minds.

Debbie Ford

The power of the human spirit inspires me. Movies, books, stories, people, anything that reminds us that we are more than just this physical body and our capacity for love and courage can bend reality.

Caity Lotz

People don't follow titles, they follow courage.

William Wells Brown

Science is imagination in the service of the verifiable truth, and that service is indeed communal. It cannot be rigidly planned. Rather, it requires freedom and courage and the plural contributions of many different kinds of people who must maintain their individuality while giving to the group.

Gerald Edelman

I became frustrated early on as a playwright by a kind of smug smallness in modern drama. There was a lack of what I now understand as courage in the work of others as well as in my own work, and I found I was mildly amused or interested by such plays but not deeply engaged or enlightened.

Ellen McLaughlin

To me, having the courage to tell your own story goes hand in hand with having the curiosity and humility to listen to others' stories.

Sarah Kay

You have to have the courage to face the unexpected. This is the difference between people who do things and people who don't dare, who don't dare to live.

Gianna Angelopoulos-Daskalaki

And as a child I was filled with passionate admiration for acts of civic courage I had seen performed by an elderly military doctor, who was a friend of my family.

Rene Cassin

I am haunted by what my life would have been had I not had the courage in my early twenties to leave Pittsburgh for New York City and really commit to being a writer. Pittsburgh is both post-industrial and provincial, and the opportunities there are limited. It would have been quite easy to simply drift through life.

Said Sayrafiezadeh

One of the hardest questions I have been asked is 'How will you manage the army if you are having menstrual cramps?' I have also been asked if I will have the courage to face criminals. My answer is that courage is not a matter of gender.

Josefina Vazquez Mota

Resignation is the courage of Christian sorrow.

Alexandre Vinet

When I met Bono at the Cannes Film festival while I was there for the film 'United 93,' he said to me, 'That's a great film, brother. Thank you for your courage in making it.' I plotzed.

David Alan Basche

Because we men have been physically stronger and more arrogant, we've influenced much of the cool stuff of the world, like basing the definition of courage on what we do on battlefields rather than on the patience or endurance or tolerance necessary for a sometimes painful daily grind that includes small children.

Clyde Edgerton

You want to shut up every Negro who has the courage to stand up and fight for the rights of his people, for the rights of workers, and I have been on many a picket line for the steelworkers too.

Paul Robeson

I have seen in the Halls of Congress more idealism, more humanness, more compassion, more profiles of courage than in any other institution that I have ever known.

Hubert H. Humphrey

He that fails in his endeavors after wealth or power will not long retain either honesty or courage.

Samuel Johnson

So the brother in black offers to these United States the source of courage that endures, and laughter.

Zora Neale Hurston

Physical courage, which despises all danger, will make a man brave in one way; and moral courage, which despises all opinion, will make a man brave in another.

Charles Caleb Colton

The courage of very ordinary people is all that stands between us and the dark.

Pam Brown

America needs jobs, smaller government, less spending and a president with the courage to offer more than yet another speech.

Rick Perry

A member must say that he is a member of the Unification Church and that he is the follower of Sun Myung Moon. If he doesn't have the courage to say it, he is not worthy of me.

Sun Myung Moon

As for courage and will - we cannot measure how much of each lies within us, we can only trust there will be sufficient to carry through trials which may lie ahead.

Andre Norton

People talk about the courage of condemned men walking to the place of execution: sometimes it needs as much courage to walk with any kind of bearing towards another person's habitual misery.

Graham Greene

Such decisions will be far reaching and difficult. But you never lacked courage in the past. Your courage is now needed for the future.

Gerry Adams

Individual courage is the only interesting thing in life.

Simone Signoret

We must remind Americans that the promise of opportunity remains unbroken - that every person in this great nation can succeed through hard work, courage and personal responsibility.

Brian Sandoval

Once I had all the facts in, I found I didn't have the

immoral courage to pull the caper. So I wrote it as a story. As a teenager, I didn't have any skills for writing as such, so it came out in 1500 words.

Theodore Sturgeon

It takes a great deal of courage to follow another person's lead.

Bill Hybels

Peace is a fragile thing. It takes courage to secure it. It takes wisdom to maintain it.

Jenny Shipley

It is so often true that whether a person carries with him an atmosphere of gloom and depression or one of confidence and courage depends on his individual outlook.

James Keller

One of the marks of a gift is to have the courage of it.

Katherine Anne Porter

I fear some of our leaders today have lost the courage to stand up. What we have now are politicians. They won't offer real plans, and only stand up when they want to blame someone else.

Susana Martinez

In short, we need to recover the courage we celebrate in our heroes, and in particular, the courage to tolerate, for the sake of a free society, a level of risk we hardly ever imagined in the past.

Daniel Dennett

My education was dominated by modernist thinkers and artists who taught me that the supreme imperative was courage to face the awful truth, to scorn the soft-minded optimism of religious and secular romantics as well as the corrupt optimism of governments, advertisers, and mechanistic or manipulative revolutionaries.

Ellen Willis

Courage is action, not talk.

Jeff Rich

The courage we desire and prize is not the courage to die decently, but to live manfully.

Thomas Carlyle

We need men with moral courage to speak and write their real thoughts, and to stand by their convictions, even to the very death.

Robert Green Ingersoll

Political courage is not political suicide.

Arnold Schwarzenegger

If we survive danger it steels our courage more than anything else.

Reinhold Niebuhr

What happened in the missile crisis in October 1962 has been prettified to make it look as if acts of courage and thoughtfulness abounded. The truth is that the whole episode was almost insane.

Noam Chomsky

Darwin gives courage to the rest of science that we shall end up understanding literally everything, springing from almost nothing - a thought extremely hard to comprehend and believe.

Richard Dawkins

Either life entails courage, or it ceases to be life.

E. M. Forster

The more wit the less courage.

Thomas Fuller

To live we must conquer incessantly, we must have the courage to be happy.

Henri Frederic Amiel

Courage in danger is half the battle.

Plautus

A wise woman knows how to summon her courage and do what is right, rather than what is easy.

Suze Orman

In all realms of life it takes courage to stretch your limits, express your power, and fulfill your potential... it's no different in the financial realm.

Suze Orman

Courage is not always about action. It takes courage to do nothing rather than do something that you do not believe in or understand.

Suze Orman

Wait for the Lord. Behave yourself manfully, and be of good courage. Do not be faithless, but stay in your place and do not turn back.

Thomas a Kempis

I find fault with my children because I like them and I want them to go places - uprightness and strength and courage and civil respect and anything that affects the probabilities of failure on the part of those that are closest to me, that concerns me - I find fault.

Branch Rickey

Every man of courage is a man of his word.

Pierre Corneille

Cowardice and courage are never without a measure of affectation. Nor is love. Feelings are never true. They play with their mirrors.

Jean Baudrillard

You cannot build character and courage by taking away a man's initiative and independence.

William J. H. Boetcker

The first thing out of Fidel Castro's mouth to me, he looked me right in the eye and said, 'You're a man of great courage.'

Jesse Ventura

When you make that crossover from life to real life, when you're not treated as a child anymore but as a man, and you are no longer given the benefit of the doubt, it takes some courage to face that.

Ricky Williams

The courage of the Syrian protesters is remarkable, for they face prison, torture, or death every time they lift a banner.

Elliott Abrams

Until the day of his death, no man can be sure of his courage.

Jean Anouilh

Never undertake anything for which you wouldn't have the courage to ask the blessings of heaven.

Georg C. Lichtenberg

Unjust. How many times I've used that word, scolded myself with it. All I mean by it now is that I don't have the final courage to say that I refuse to preside over violations against myself, and to hell with justice.

Lillian Hellman

It takes some courage to write fiction about politically controversial topics. The dread is you'll be labeled a political writer.

Barbara Kingsolver

I have no physical courage, I've asked for a double.

Catherine Deneuve

When I first started writing songs and being very explicit, it was hard, but one of the main things people respond to in my writing is that 'just say it' attitude of my songs. There really is nothing personal or private; it's all universal, if you can just find the courage to be open about your life.

Ani DiFranco

I had to find the courage to turn my life around.

Nikki Sixx

There's only one thing worse than a man who doesn't have

strong likes and dislikes, and that's a man who has strong likes and dislikes without the courage to voice them.

Tony Randall

War is fear cloaked in courage.

William Westmoreland

You can do anything if you set your mind to it. Look out for kids, help them dream and be inspired. We teach calculus in schools, but I believe the most important formula is courage plus dreams equals success.

Marlee Matlin

Enthusiasm is a form of social courage.

Gretchen Rubin

With enough courage, you can do without a reputation.

Margaret Mitchell

And I think most people in this country want to see a

president that's got the courage to say we're going to cut the tax burden, and reduce the regulatory climate, and we're going to get Americans working.

Rick Perry

If one girl with courage is a revolution, imagine what feats we can achieve together.

Queen Rania of Jordan

Faith in God... produces character; character will produce courage, courage to face the challenges of the day.

Kirk Cameron

No, I am not a homosexual. If I were a homosexual, I would hope I would have the courage to say so. What's cruel is that you are forcing me to say I am not a homosexual. This means you are putting homosexuals down. I don't want to do that.

Ed Koch

The truth won't set us free - until we develop the skills and the habit and the talent and the moral courage to use it.

Margaret Heffernan

When I write, what I long for is not more realism or fiction but more courage. That's what I always find myself short on and what I have to struggle to achieve in order that the work might live.

Junot Diaz

In acting, there's a type of courage you're recognized for all the time. You lose 100 pounds and play a guy with AIDS, and you get rewarded. But, in life, doing what is courageous is quiet, and no one knows about it. Courage is someone making sacrifices for their family or making selfless decisions for what they hope or feel.

Rob Lowe

A statesman wants courage and a statesman wants vision; but believe me, after six months' experience, he wants first, second, third and all the time - patience.

Stanley Baldwin

Courage is always rewarded.

Kenny Loggins

Australia is a nation of compassion. Courage and compassion. And the third of these great values: resilience.

Kevin Rudd

I try to be a truthful artist and I try to show a level of courage. I enjoy that. I'm a messenger.

Jeff Koons

Remember that the good angels do what they can to preserve men from sin and obtain God's honor. But they do not lose courage when men fail.

Saint Ignatius

Poe had this curious kind of alchemical courage, where he took all the terrible things and terrors that happened in his life, all this shame and fear and pain, and turned them into great works of art. He was a complex, brilliant person who was just wired too tight.

John Cusack

It is the mainspring of life, courage. And courage has many faces.

Oriana Fallaci

In my experience as CEO, I found that the most important decisions tested my courage far more than my intelligence.

Ben Horowitz

Without strength and courage it's really hard to perform at the highest levels of international figure skating, because you're alone on the ice and you only have seven minutes over two nights to prove yourself.

Scott Hamilton

Real courage is knowing what faces you and knowing how to face it.

Timothy Dalton

I never modeled myself after anyone. The person who had most influence on me was my mother, but it was really for her strength and courage more than her style, even though she had a lot of style. In a weird way, looking at pictures of me when I was 17 or 18, I was dressing the same way. I haven't changed very much.

Diane von Furstenberg

What is more mortifying than to feel that you have missed the plum for want of courage to shake the tree?

Logan Pearsall Smith

If the anti-Christian agenda will say, 'Here's your identity, you're an evolved amoeba who ought to just go do whatever you want and don't let anybody tell you different,' then they can get you to throw your faith, your character, your courage, and your liberty right out the window.

Kirk Cameron

TV is so different from the movies. It takes a lot of stamina because you work such long hours. It is really challenging. You are learning the next day's lines while you are shooting today's scenes. I found courage I never realised I had. I hope to do more.

Sharon Stone

I want to thank the Academy for its courage and generosity.

Elia Kazan

Keep courage. Whatever you do, do not feel sorry for yourself. You will win in a great age of opportunity.

Richard L. Evans

Each of us has an inner dream that we can unfold if we will just have the courage to admit what it is. And the faith to trust our own admission. The admitting is often very difficult.

Julia Cameron

I hope America can also be the cultural leader of the world, and use this frontier spirit to lead and show others that we need courage to go places where we have not gone before.

Tadao Ando

My sword I give to him that shall succeed me in my pilgrimage, and my courage and skill to him that can get it.

John Bunyan

What I've always said is that I'm opposed to institutional racism, and I would've, had I've been alive at the time, I think, had the courage to march with Martin Luther King to overturn institutional racism, and I see no place in our society for institutional racism.

Rand Paul

Two European nations emerged with credit from the Iraq disaster: France and Germany. Both had the courage to withstand the Bush administration and oppose the U.S.-led invasion.

Martin Jacques

All my life I had feared to-morrow, until I decided to have faith and to live to-day in courage.

Vash Young

There is no glory in war, yet from the blackness of its history, there emerge vivid colours of human character and courage. Those who risked their lives to help their friends.

Silvia Cartwright

The thing is, when I feel like I have to lose weight, the opposite happens. I remember stuffing loads of chocolate on the plane to the shoot, and I thought, 'Why don't you have the courage to show up in a body that's natural, not overly worked out?'

Geri Halliwell

If you are a superstar, or whatever you want to call yourself, a person who's had outrageous success, and you decide to go indie and tell the record companies to screw themselves? That takes a certain amount of courage. And bullheadedness, really.

Daryl Hall

Courage is heartworth making itself felt in deeds. It never waits for chances; it makes chances.

George Matthew Adams

Everybody's opinion is equally valid, and I feel like everybody should have an opportunity to speak out, and everyone should have the courage to speak out.

Michael Franti

That's what acting is - it's about... having the courage to allow your audience into the private moments of your characters' lives.

Kerry Washington

I'm not going to be bullied or pushed around by the group of the day. You've got to have political courage. You've got to have your own inner beliefs.

Madeleine M. Kunin

If his presidency is to represent the full power of the idea that black Americans are just like everyone else - fully human and fully capable of intellect, courage and patriotism - then Barack Obama has to be subject to the same rough and tumble of political criticism experienced by his predecessors.

Juan Williams

Hire sales people who are really smart problem solvers, but lack courage, hunger and competitiveness, and your company will go out of business.

Ben Horowitz

I've always been independent. I've always had courage. But I didn't always own my diabetes.

Mary Tyler Moore

I do get scared, but I think - like it says in another book I've read - feel the fear and do it anyway. I try to have courage, pray a little bit and work through it. I'd rather try, even if I fail.

Geri Halliwell

Ofttimes the test of courage becomes rather to live than to die.

Vittorio Alfieri

A man of courage flees forward, in the midst of new things.

Jacques Maritain

It shouldn't take extreme courage and a willingness to go to prison for decades or even life to blow the whistle on bad government acts done in secret. But it does. And that is an immense problem for democracy, one that all journalists should be united in fighting.

Glenn Greenwald

One of the things that makes Hamlet unique among Shakespeare's characters is his courage to face up to the darker elements of his personality.

Kenneth Branagh

I think that people need to have the courage of their convictions and not be trying to fool people into thinking that they've changed overnight.

Chris Bell

Prime Minister Sharon, Prime Minister Abbas, I urge you today to end the designs of those who seek destruction, annihilation and occupation, and I urge you to have the will and the courage to begin to realize our dreams of peace, prosperity and coexistence.

Abdallah II of Jordan

The things I do, I do from the heart and out of love and respect for our planet and all living things. And I draw my courage from my love for justice and truth, and I calm my fears by comforting those who are more scared than me. And I try to do my best to make the world a better place, one small action at a time, as good as I can.

Q'orianka Kilcher

Well, number one I like dancing. Number two I knew it would be challenging because I had never done this type of dance before. I always wanted to and I happened to have the courage to go out there and give it my best shot.

Evander Holyfield

Nobody has yet proven that taking a chance and doing something unique that an audience isn't used to is a bad idea. What the theater lacks is that kind of courage.

Harold Prince

It takes courage to know when you ought to be afraid.

James A. Michener

My talent is such that no undertaking, however vast in size... has ever surpassed my courage.

Peter Paul Rubens

It has been my honor to support and work with President Barack Obama, a man who has brought courage and character to the presidency. President Obama's strength of character leads him to do the right thing, even when it isn't the easy thing.

Harry Reid

A leader must have the courage to act against an expert's advice.

James Callaghan

When somebody who makes movies for a living - either as an actor, writer, producer or director - lives to be a certain age, you have to admire them. It is an act of courage to make a film - a courage for which you are not prepared in the rest of life. It is very hard and very destructive. But we do it because we love it.

John Carpenter

I think a lot of people may have a unique insight or some idea that they feel could be a great solution for a particular problem, but for some reason never have a chance to try or never have the courage or maybe the self-doubt. Really, it's best just to remain naive and continue to work on things and see if people have the same problems.

Chad Hurley

I am always naturally drawn to heroines that have human flaws because I enjoy people that have lived their life with courage and make big successes and big failures.

Romola Garai

Have the courage to face a difficulty lest it kick you harder than you bargain for.

Stanislaus I

Everybody, even me, sometimes had to compromise on something, doing things we know to be wrong, and this happens doing whatever job in the world. But a singer must have the courage of saying no.

Jose Carreras

My aunt is the director of the acapella group Black Voices.

I was so struck by them as a child. They sang with such passion and conviction. By the time I turned 15, I had plucked up the courage to ask if I could join the group. Acapella is a different discipline from singing with an accompaniment - it is much more exposed.

Laura Mvula

Throughout the history of our young nation, we have seen our military go bravely into battle, armed with courage and willing to make the ultimate sacrifice.

John M. McHugh

I wish we lived in a society that made it safe and provided the courage for everyone to come out.

Judith Light

What you learn from studying acting is that you have to have the courage to just make strong choices.

Sarah Rafferty

I could never muster the courage to speak to girls in my college in Pune. Most of them were Parsis and spoke

English. I came from a village and could barely converse in English.

Sharad Pawar

My intent is not to inflame Muslims but to entertain readers of great thrillers. At the end of the day, I want people to see a good protagonist struggle against serious odds and do so with courage and honor and integrity.

Brad Thor

The world will step aside for nearly anyone who has the courage of his of her opinions.

George Weinberg

Freedom is a system based on courage.

Charles Peguy

Moses became America's true founding father because he evangelized action; he justified risk. He gave ordinary people the courage to live with uncertainty.

Bruce Feiler

I've always been inspired by artists who have shown musical and intellectual curiosity and the courage to take risks.

Renee Fleming

Heroes to me are guys that sit in libraries. They absorb knowledge and then the risks they take are calculated on the basis of the courage it took to become replete with knowledge.

William Hurt

Intellectuals try to keep going. But their situation is very difficult. Those who have had the courage to voice their opposition have often paid a very high price.

Tahar Ben Jelloun

I can make a virtue of slapdash. Slapdash can give you courage.

Sally Phillips

How many women have the courage to start properly with a

cold, cold bath early in the morning? I jump in, throw the water, cold as ice, and after the first plunge I am happy.

Anna Held

It takes courage to stay young, to make your enthusiasms work for you. Don't let anyone drag you down.

Ken Adam

Martin Luther King, Jr. Day is a time to honor the greatest champion of racial equality who taught a nation - through compassion and courage - about democracy, nonviolence and racial justice.

Mark Pryor

Political courage requires clarity.

Joe Klein

Pride is tough. You go to high school, and its 'pride,' 'courage;' it's all these types of words that we use to motivate us. I don't think there's anywhere in the Scriptures through the saints' lives where pride was ever a positive characteristic of anybody.

Troy Polamalu

For as long as this nation has known war, we have embraced the heroes it has produced. Americans have rightfully noted the honor and nobility of courage under hostile fire and thanked those who perished in their defense.

James T. Walsh

There can be a fundamental gulf of gracelessness in a human heart which neither our love nor our courage can bridge.

Patrick Campbell

You live with the fear people might find out. Then you actually have the courage to tell people and they go, I don't think you are gay. It's enough to drive you crazy.

Portia de Rossi

You always remember the delicacy of the work you do on a new play - the delicacy and the rigor and the courage.

Lindsay Duncan

Where a man's strength and courage is tested most is in the way that he treats women - the way that he loves.

John Eldredge

President Obama and our all-of-the-above energy strategy is the real deal. We are proud of the fact that we are importing less oil than at any time in modern history, and it has been because of the president's vision and courage.

Ken Salazar

Because at bottom, I'm interested in fear, and in courage and cowardice and these are easier to get at through fiction, where you can enter people's heads.

Kevin Patterson

I'll know how to die with courage; that is easier than living.

Georg Buchner

I admired Eugene McCarthy's courage and although I left his Senate staff after four years to accept a job as the researcher on the editorial page of the 'Washington Post,' I remained an admirer.

Kitty Kelley

I adore themes of hope and courage and the ways we find meaning through suffering.

Ruta Sepetys

Whenever I see John Lewis, I invariably say, 'Thank you.' And I will never stop. I don't know how he's still standing, because what he endured took courage and strength that I don't know that I have.

Don Lemon

I'm a writer of faith who worries about the intolerance of religion. I look at the past and fear we haven't learned from it. I believe that humanity is capable of evil as well as great acts of courage and goodness. I have hope. Deep down, I believe in the human spirit, although sometimes that belief is shaken.

Julianna Baggott

War criminals in the U.S. and Israel are not punished: no

international court has the courage to put them on trial.

Nawal El Saadawi

Without white South Africa realizing what it had done - and on the basis of that realization having the courage to ask for forgiveness - there can really be no significant movement.

Athol Fugard

Courage to continue comes from deeper sources than outward results.

Kenneth L. Pike

For millions, Roger Ebert will be remembered as a writer and television personality who brought a sense of passion and excellence to his craft. For me, he is a man who fused joy and courage as few others ever have. My life was enriched by having such a friend; it is poorer for losing such a friend.

Jeff Greenfield

Most of the good executives do pretty well. Because to be a

good executive you have to be strong, and you have to have a simple attribute that people have forgotten about - courage.

John Milius

What makes America amazing is that there have always been men and women of courage who were willing to think more about the future of their children and grandchildren than they did about their own political careers.

Scott Walker

If you set as your goal to roll back the size of government, you have an obligation to answer the tough questions and show real courage, not just appeal to ideology. Treat the voters like adults.

Brian Baird

The word courage - God, I love that word. Words are so important to me.

Peter Fonda

Those who are rooted in the depths that are eternal and

unchangeable and who rely on unshakeable principles, face change full of courage, courage based on faith.

Emily Greene Balch

I see courage everywhere I go in Africa.

John Prendergast

I've decided to run for the U.S. Senate because I believe Wisconsin families need a senator who will work hard to deliver results for the middle class - a leader with the courage to do what's right, no matter how tough the odds or how powerful the special interests we have to fight.

Tammy Baldwin

The qualities of an exceptional cook are akin to those of a successful tightrope walker: an abiding passion for the task, courage to go out on a limb and an impeccable sense of balance.

Bryan Q. Miller

California is a place of invention, a place of courage, a place of vision, a place of the future. People who made

California what it is were willing to take risks, think outside convention and build.

Nicolas Berggruen

Young men and young women, full of courage, originality, and genius, are everywhere to be met with.

Frank Crowninshield

I believe the biggest challenge is just getting the courage to try something different or new. Try to forget the stereotype in your mind. Yoga is for everyone - children, athletes, moms, dads, accountants, truck drivers, even country stars.

Kristian Bush

When I was growing up in Virginia, the Civil War was presented to me as glorious with dramatic courage and military honor. Later, I realized how death was central to the reality. It was at the core of women's lives. It's what they talked about most.

Drew Gilpin Faust

We had every problems starting a big top could have. The

tent fell down on the first day. We had problems getting people into the shows. It was only with the courage and arrogance of youth that we survived.

Guy Laliberte

Paul persuaded me to join the band. I would never have had the courage otherwise. It was fun at the beginning. We were playing just for fun, with Paul's group.

Linda McCartney

My first and most loved real novel was 'Little Women.' I identified with the Jo character even though we were opposites. Jo was very strong-minded and brave, and I was shy and kind of a wuss, everyplace but in my own home. I wanted to be Jo. She was my alter ego. I think reading that book gave me courage.

Rhea Perlman

My big inspiration for hope is the courage that I read about from people from all over the world, or that I see on a daily basis from the kids I get to work with.

Morley

As a gay Jewish white South African, I belong to quite a lot of minority groups. You constantly have to question who you are, what you are and whether you have the courage to be who you are.

Antony Sher

But after this natural burst of indignation, no man of sense, courage, or prudence will waste his time or his strength in retrospective reproaches or repinings.

Robert Peel

If I am to be known for anything, I would like it to be for encouraging Canadians, for knowing a little bit about their daily, extraordinary courage. And for wanting that courage to be recognized.

Romeo LeBlanc

Probably most dying patients, even when suffering greatly, would choose to live as long as possible. That courage and grace should be protected and honored, and we should put every effort into treating their symptoms.

Marcia Angell

Men who live valiantly and die nobly have a strength and a courage from the eternal Father.

Josephus Daniels

We all have ambitions, but only the few achieve. A man thinks of a good thing and says: 'Now if I only had the money I'd put that through.' The word 'if' was a dent in his courage. With character fully established, his plan well thought out, he had only to go to those in command of capital and it would have been forthcoming.

Douglas Fairbanks

The right response to the non-problem of global warming is to have the courage to do nothing.

Christopher Monckton

At the end of the day, New Yorkers need a mayor who understands the problems they face, brings a smart plan and good people to the table, and, more than anything, has the independence, courage and conviction to do the right thing.

Sal Albanese

Having the courage to say no when all your friends are saying yes is one of the most difficult things you'll ever have to do. Doing it, however, is one of the biggest charges you can ever make to your personal battery. I call this 'won't power.'

Sean Covey

I see courage everywhere I go in Africa. Fearless human rights activists in Darfur. Women peace advocates in eastern Congo. Former child soldiers in Northern Uganda who now are helping other former child soldiers return to civilian life.

John Prendergast

Discover your own style. Don't try to repeat what has already been written - have the courage to do your own thing and don't be afraid to do something different.

Cecelia Ahern

They put me in a harness, like a horse, to learn the back somersault. It was weird up there when I put on that harness for the first time. The courage came with practice.

Donald O'Connor

Iwas not a reader at all, not until I discovered 'The Hobbit.'
That changed my life. It gave me the courage to read. It led
me to the 'Lord of the Rings' series. And once I'd read that,
I knew I could read anything because I had just read
thousands of pages.

Richard Paul Evans

With Pearl Jam, everybody is so good at what they do, it's
hard to get up the courage to say, Can I sing this part, or, I
want to play guitar. I feel like I have more courage to do
that.

Jeff Ament

My main trick is to work with amazing people. It's a long
and twisty journey, and you need people that really are
amazing and have this rare gift of honesty and courage and
really open up.

Lucy Walker

It takes a lot of courage as an actor to take time off for
family. But family is everything.

Shari Sebbens

Confronting and undermining the narratives and ideas of extremism must therefore be one of our key tasks. To do this, we must retain the courage of our convictions in the face of extremism.

Jonas Gahr Store

Remember in 1973 the same science chatter said that the coming Ice Age is going to occur, we're going to lose millions of people. And the politicians knew how to solve it, they just didn't have the courage to solve it; they were going to put coal dust on the Arctic.

Don Young

Necessity does the work of courage.

Nicholas M. Butler

The quality that defines us as Americans is the courage to respond to being hit. The courage to root out and destroy the killers. And, most importantly, the courage to hold on to our values and protect our hard-won freedoms while doing it.

Nick Clooney

I think the moments that are difficult for anybody are when you see what your life could be, if only you had the courage to take the steps needed.

John Slattery

If you can find the courage, if you have in your heart even the slightest bit of rebellion against injustice, maybe you can channel that and become a leader.

Cherry Jones

When I became a parent and hit my thirties, I got my hands on an acoustic guitar. I started writing quiet, simple songs at home and, with a little encouragement, I got more courage and found my voice. I have people and movements who have inspired me to carry on, but I try to write about things I know, nothing too complicated, really.

Withered Hand

The joy of style lies not in how we look to other people, but in how we look to ourselves - and the most memorable and beautiful outfits are simply those that, in some rare moment of joy, we found the courage to share with the world.

Simon Van Booy

I think the Iraqi people have shown extraordinary patience and courage in the last few months. They have really put a political system on the way to success, to a real democracy here.

Paul Bremer

Give the people not hell, but hope and courage.

John Murray

We can never intimidate and discourage the people who voice their words with courage. The essence of freedom rests precisely here - in the freedom of expression of the people. And we must protect it.

Tsakhiagiin Elbegdorj

The single outstanding exception was the broad yet precise mandate communicated by the General Assembly in 1946 to prepare as soon as possible the Charter of Human Rights which the San Francisco Conference had not had the time or the courage to draw up.

Rene Cassin

Courage is rightly esteemed the first of human qualities - because it is the quality which guarantees all others.

Joseph Chamberlain

Morality may consist solely in the courage of making a choice.

Leon Blum

There's no mystique to acting. It's only common sense - and a bit of courage.

Bill Hunter

It's up to the courage of the filmmakers to make art in cinema, not just business. John was rejected by studios, he borrowed money and did movies with his own money. You're either courageous or not. You have to find a way.

Ben Gazzara

Even within the last three or four years, I have a greater

ability to communicate, I think. I have more courage to show the stuff... And it does take courage.

Barbara Cook

You need the commitment of people that aren't worried about that next election, who are going to do the right thing and worry about the next generation. It's called political courage. And I can tell you, with me, you don't have to ask whether I have political courage.

Jeff Fitzgerald

Sarah Vaughan is one of my greatest heroes. She personifies what an artist is all about, taking risks, daring to go beyond the boundaries of safety and convention. It takes courage to share your vulnerability.

Claron McFadden

But we got up there and decided to stick to this mix of power chords and funk and that's where it really started for us. In having the courage to take that decision. To take a gamble not just with our music but our lives.

Michael Hutchence

As a young man, I felt a need to communicate with somebody or something, but it seemed in my own particular environment that that wasn't an option. On the other hand, I probably lacked the courage to do so, even if it was an option.

Nick Tosches

At the same time, I would add that the American people have a lot of courage.

Tadao Ando

I don't know what kind of courage it took thousands of years ago, but I know how courageous women need to be today.

Beth Moore

The 'Bird's Nest' National Stadium, which I helped to conceive, is designed to embody the Olympic spirit of 'fair competition.' It tells people that freedom is possible but needs fairness, courage and strength.

Ai Weiwei

You must have love as the core; it takes courage to be willing to constantly tell the truth to each other and risk letting the relationship go.

Kenny Loggins

Farrah Fawcett had courage, she had strength, and she had faith.

Jaclyn Smith

I know that throughout their history, the people of the United States defended their freedom, their liberty, their justice, and their rights - if need be - with their lives. I think their courage is so admirable.

Lee Myung-bak

Now that I've got some films under my belt, I have the courage of my convictions regarding acting. It gives me a leg to stand on.

Mira Sorvino

Through the inspiration of Vaclav's words, the courage of his dissidence and the integrity of his leadership,

Czechoslovakia successfully transitioned from an authoritarian state to a free democracy at the heart of Europe.

Michael D. Higgins

Courage ought to have eyes as well as arms.

Henry George Bohn

Fashion should not be expected to serve in the stead of courage or character.

Loretta Young

It takes a certain courage and a certain greatness to be truly base.

Jean Anouilh

What separated Ed Murrow from the rest of the pack was courage.

Dan Rather

The Brazilian poet Vinicius de Moraes wrote that beauty is fundamental. Well, with the poet's permission, so is courage.

Tina Brown

Art, it seems to me, doesn't need freedom so much as it needs courage and love - some would call it 'soul' or 'Eros.'

Michael Leunig

Daniel Ellsberg showed tremendous courage back in the '70s.

Barton Gellman

Readers of fiction read, I think, for a deeper embrace of the world, of reality. And that's brave. I never get over being thankful for that - for the courage of my readers.

Barbara Kingsolver

Today, because of President Obama's courage, kids can stay on their parent's plan until they are 26. Insurers cannot kick you off your policy because you have hit your limit. They will not be able to deny you because you have a preexisting condition.

Rahm Emanuel

I want to find the candidates who understand the principles of American exceptionalism and have the character, the courage, and the confidence to actually lead the greatest nation in the world.

Jim DeMint

In 1984, showing extraordinary courage, a group of Guatemalan wives, mothers and other relatives of disappeared people banded together to form the Mutual Support Group for the Appearance Alive of Our Relatives.

Stephen Kinzer

Acting is really about having the courage to fail in front of people.

Adam Driver

What we need is some people to stand up with the courage of their convictions, to do what they promised when they ran for election, and fight to stop Obamacare.

Jim DeMint

You have to have courage to look back and be honest about your own drama.

Estelle

For me, it's not necessarily interesting to play a strong, fearless woman. It's interesting to play a woman who is terrified and then overcomes that fear. It's about the journey. Courage is not the absence of fear, it's overcoming it.

Natalie Dormer

You can think what you like of Madonna - about her political choices and her PR - but you have to respect her courage not to let the critics stop her exploring her potential.

Natalie Dormer

I have given up the idea that there is an opposition-free church out there. But I have gained something else - an appreciation for the gift of opposition. When it comes, I learn something about my motives. When it comes, I get to test my courage.

John Ortberg

Watching 'Girls' has just given me renewed courage.

Caitlin Moran

Deep Throat's information, and in my view, courage, allowed the newspaper to use what he knew and suspected.

Bob Woodward

When I was straight, I had the courage and energy to become an actress. I owe my career to my will to stop using.

Kirstie Alley

You have to do what you need to do as an artist. You have to have that courage.

Liz Phair

Courage is the essential element in any great public man or

woman.

Paul Johnson

If you see a person who's insecure and covers it up, it can be quite a problem. But the person who is insecure and shows you is quite appealing. They give you just the courage to drop your defenses.

Isabella Rossellini

I'm fascinated how often and with what whole-heartedness people will risk their lives to perform acts of courage, sacrifice, and compassion for total strangers.

Diane Ackerman

Obama wants to be thought of as the president who freed us from foreign oil. But if he doesn't show some political courage, he may well be remembered as the president who cooked the planet.

Jeff Goodell

The President regards the Japanese as a brave people; but courage, though useful in time of war, is subordinate to knowledge of arts; hence, courage without such knowledge is not to be highly esteemed.

Townsend Harris

Since I was a little girl, I have witnessed the strength and courage that energized my mother, who left every sorrow and pain in the past, who would work unyieldingly to obtain her goals, who was the great warrior from whom I learned all the values that are today fundamental pillars of my every day.

Thalia

When I moved to the East Village in the late seventies, I wanted to be a street performer, so I practiced daily. I never did work up the skills or the courage to perform on the street, though.

Steve Buscemi

As long as the opposition believes the world will stand with Ukraine's democrat reformers, they will have the leverage and the courage to establish a legitimate republic under the leadership of Viktor Yushchenko.

Bob Schaffer

The most important thing for me was to never, ever, ever deny it. But I didn't really have the courage to talk about it. I was thinking, The people who need to know I'm gay know.

Portia de Rossi

The one thing I learned the most about acting is it takes a tremendous amount of courage to go there and stand still. It takes courage and guts to step out of your mind frame and depict something.

Carson Daly

He's nice enough not to want to be associated with a nasty remark but not nice enough not to make it. Lacking the courage of one's nastiness does not make one nice.

Michael Kinsley

Yes, you must have the courage of being free.

Jose Carreras

I believe in a world where there are no heroes, and I've read and know humanity a lot. There are moments that I admire in a person courage, intellect, hard work. These are the qualities I admire in an intellectual, in a writer, and there are so many people who have these things.

Orhan Pamuk

I know what real courage is, and I understand true compassion.

Mo Yan

For many years I wanted to do a film, but I never had the courage to clear my desk and say, 'OK I'll take a year off and do a film.'

Anton Corbijn

I don't - you know, I'm very disillusioned with our political system. If we don't wake up in America and realize that we have to vote out of our courage and integrity for candidates who reflect our own beatitudes, and not the beatitudes of the war machine and the corporations, we are - we're doomed.

Cindy Sheehan

I admire people who come to politics because it takes a lot of courage to be in politics in India.

Shekhar Kapur

I have a huge political interest. I just wish I had the courage to come into politics in India.

Shekhar Kapur

I think we need people with stronger ideals than John Kerry or Bill Clinton. I think we need people with more courage and vision.

Octavia E. Butler

It was actually a women's writing group I belonged to in graduate school that gave me the courage to move from poetry to fiction.

Mary Gordon

In this work I have received the opposition of a number of men who only advocate the unobtainable because the immediately possible is beyond their moral courage, administrative ability, and their political prescience.

John Burns

I love Joan Collins. She's a wonderful lady. She has such courage. She's such a good actress.

Robert Wagner

I used to be so intimidated by spin classes. I'd always go by and see people on their bikes looking so intense. But one day my sister and I worked up the courage to go in, and now we're hooked!

Alexa Vega

I remember being a teenager and seeing Seymour Cassel across a crowded room and being incredibly star struck, and not having the courage to say, 'Hello.'

Ira Sachs

I took my courage in both hands and went to the Laundromat to do my washing. I had to use three machines.

Julie Doucet

It is quite true that women like courage, and that boldness often goes a long way; but it is questionable whether with high-bred natures a subdued, quiet, and delicate manner does not go still further.

Richard Jefferies

We simply do not understand our place in the universe and have not the courage to admit it.

Barry Lopez

That was the fun of acting, being a blank canvas you could transform into the character - Indian princess, 20s vamp, Mother Courage, Oxford don, 94-year-old wife.

Diana Quick

When finally I mustered the courage to tell a novelist friend that I was talking to editors about a biography, her reply was, 'Oh, that's okay. That's not a real book.'

Stacy Schiff

The people of South Carolina support conservatives who are trying to push real change, and the people of South

Carolina expect their presidential candidates to back them up when they show courage.

Nikki Haley

I feel like Obama in a way. His idea that hope means not shrinking from a fight; it's the courage to reach for something. My music is that. Those are principles I try to embody.

Q-Tip

I have decided to make a personal message to David Haye. I want him to fight me, to be a man. I wish there will be enough excitement, pressure and courage for David Haye to fight me.

Wladimir Klitschko

One of the things your unconscious mind does for you - and it's a great gift - is it gives you extra courage to view the outer world and it does that by giving you an extra-special view of yourself.

Leonard Mlodinow

Before I begin talking about the threats we face, the vulnerabilities that we have, and frankly the courage of the men and women in uniform that stand in harm's way on behalf of a very grateful Nation, let me first honor the sacrifices of September 11.

Zach Wamp

I'm still shy - I'm no good at my children's parent-teacher conferences, and I'm slowly learning how to ask for what I want. But I now know that I have a reserve of courage to draw upon when I really need it. There's nothing that I'm too scared to have a go at.

Emily Mortimer

Howard Dean has been successful because he was clear in his opposition to the war. People appreciate a politician with the courage to say, I oppose this war.

Bianca Jagger

If the City Council wants to hold the police accountable, it has the subpoena power and oversight responsibility to do so. They don't have the courage to do it.

Sal Albanese

With Pearl Jam, everybody is so good at what they do, it's hard to get up the courage to say, 'Can I sing this part,' or, 'I want to play guitar.'

Jeff Ament

When I was at Brown, I wanted to write the great American novel, but I was too scared to take a creative course. I signed up for one, got in, and just didn't have the courage to go. I was a tremendously shy person, almost pathologically shy. The thought of peers critiquing my work - oh, God.

Nathaniel Philbrick

Sadly, far too many politicians in Washington lack the courage to do something to fix our problems. They are worried about the political implications of making the hard choices we so desperately need to cut spending and shrink government.

Matt Salmon

In the inhalation and exhalation there is an energy and a lively divine spirit, since He, through his spirit supports the breath of life, giving courage to the people who are in the earth and spirit to those who walk on it.

Michael Servetus

I have three favorite politicians: Reagan, Truman, and Bobby Kennedy - Bobby for showing remarkable political courage despite being loathed by many on both sides.

Joe Scarborough

I started to send my work to journals when I was 26, which was just a question of when I got the courage up. They were mostly journals I had been reading for the previous six or seven years.

Marilyn Hacker

If we can't have the courage to tell our constituents, hey, we've got to cut back, then if we can point to something and say, I would like to vote for more benefits for you, but this balanced budget amendment or statutory spending cap or whatever the device is, is preventing me from doing it.

Jeff Flake

Let me start with Yahoo. As we meet today, a Chinese citizen who had the courage to speak his mind on the Internet is in prison because Yahoo chose to share his name and address with the Chinese Government.

Tom Lantos

What I do know is that writing is the thing I am best at, and I don't have the stomach, the ability, the strength or the courage to enter the political arena. And I think writing can be a political act, if only to let those people accountable know they are being watched. Literature can be a conscience.

Miguel Syjuco

I think what I would say to my younger self, and probably to younger, just starting-out writers is that a lot of times you're just afraid to put yourself out there, and it's uncomfortable because it's working up the courage to do something, to push yourself to do those things.

Carol Leifer

Courage is just fear plus prayers plus understanding.

Eddie Albert

I like so much wearing heels, legs look so much better,

everything looks better. But it's only recently I've had the courage to do that.

Blanka Vlasic

I emphasize... that the Harrimans showed great courage and loyalty and confidence in us, because three or four of us were really running the business, the day to day business.

Prescott Bush

Just two weeks ago, millions of Iraqis defied the threats of terrorists and went to the polls to determine their own future. I congratulate the Iraqi people for the courage they've shown in making these elections so successful.

Bill Frist

It takes far less courage to kill yourself than it takes to make yourself wake up one more time. It's harder to stay where you are than to get out. For everyone but you, that is.

Judith Rossner

Courage is just fear, plus prayers, plus understanding.

Edward Albert

Someone once told me the one thread that runs through them all is a premium on personal courage - not intellectual courage, but just plain physical courage.

Walter Lord

I know this president. And I can tell you that he cares deeply about the next generation of young women in this country - his daughters, and everyone's daughters. President Obama had the courage to stand with Sandra Fluke. Without hesitation, he defended her right to tell her story.

Nancy Keenan

It is up to African leaders to show their will and political courage in order to assure that this new pan-African institution becomes an efficient instrument and not a place for endless discussions.

Omar Bongo

So much inspires me. People living their lives with courage, beauty of all kinds, nature in all its aspects, people I love and people I hardly know, and, of course, other poets.

Ellen Bass

When I was 16 the first girl I had a crush on wasn't interested at all. I liked her from afar for ages, and when I eventually got the courage and told her, and she wasn't into me.

Luke Pasqualino

The memoirs that have come out of Africa are sometimes startlingly beautiful, often urgent, and essentially life-affirming, but they are all performances of courage and honesty.

Alexandra Fuller

Some people call it the 'Al Jazeera spirit' - courage, re-thinking authority, giving a voice to the voiceless. We have never been favored by the authority. The human being is the center of our editorial policy. We are not a TV station that rushes after stars, big names, press conferences, hand-shake journalism.

Wadah Khanfar

Traveling gives you some perspective of what the rest of

the world is like. I think that having the courage to step out of the norm is the most important thing.

Meghan Markle

It may not be the most popular but there is a place for it. I think about the kind of music I love, acoustic, melodic, and I guess it kind of took a bit of courage on my part to think I could be one of those songwriters.

Helen Slater

I want to work as hard as I can. But I also want six kids! It takes a lot of courage as an actor to take time off for family. But family is everything.

Shari Sebbens

We know the Republicans are happy to keep the country in the dark, and if we Democrats are to recapture the power necessary to assert our values, we must find the energy, courage, creativity and unity to map out a brighter day for the people we sincerely want to serve.

John Yarmuth

I remember having friends in high school that did the theater department stuff, and I always wanted to try it but never had the guts to. I was the class clown but could never really build up the courage to try it. I took one acting class and really enjoyed it.

Robert Buckley

When I began work on my first book, 'The River of Doubt,' which tells the story of Theodore Roosevelt's 1914 descent of an unmapped river in the Amazon rainforest, I thought of it as a tale of adventure, exploration and extraordinary courage.

Candice Millard

I think we women underrate ourselves when it comes to our courage and strength.

Judith McNaught

I learned that Congress is a place with more heart than courage; there are more good souls in Washington than brave ones. I learned that the whole is not always the sum of its parts: that what you put in doesn't always match what you get out.

Joaquin Castro

You'll notice that my books offer great variety. Some are for adults, some for children and some for teens. There are mysteries, historical novels, picture books, love stories and stories of crisis and courage.

Sonia Levitin

www.ingramcontent.com/pod-product-compliance
Lightning Source LLC
Chambersburg PA
CBHW070644290526
45790CB00001B/186